The A to Z Guide to Soul-Inspiring Leadership

Jaime –
Thanks for being
here today!

CAROL-ANN HAMILTON
JAMES NORRIE

THE A TO Z GUIDE

To **Soul-Inspiring Leadership**

Belleville, Ontario, Canada

The A to Z Guide to Soul-Inspiring Leadership

First printing November 2003
Second printing November 2004

National Library of Canada Cataloguing in Publication

Hamilton, Carol-Ann, 1958-
The A to Z guide to soul inspiring leadership / Carol-Ann Hamilton and James Norrie.

ISBN 1-55306-603-0.--ISBN 1-55306-605-7 (LSI ed.)

1. Leadership. I. Norrie, James, 1965- II. Title.

HD57.7.H348 2003 658.4'092 C2003-904208-1

For more information or to order additional copies, please contact:

Internet: www.soul-inspiring-leadership.com

Epic Press is an imprint of *Essence Publishing*. For more information, contact:

Phone: 1-800-238-6376
Internet: www.essencegroup.com

Printed in Canada
by

Table of Contents

Acknowledgements 7
Preface 13

Acknowledgement 19
Balance 29
Courage 39
Diversity 48
Emotions 59
Fun 69
Grace 78
Heart 86
Imagination 94
Jobs 103
Knowing 112
Learning 121

Maturity .133
Nurturing .144
Obsolescence .152
Passion .160
Questions .171
Relationships .181
Servant Leadership .191
Technology .201
Upheaval .209
Values .217
Wealth .226
X-traordinary .234
Yearning .243
Zap .252

The Nine Simple Leadership Equations
Number One .23
Number Two .56
Number Three .105
Number Four .129
Number Five .134
Number Six .165
Number Seven .203
Number Eight .220
Number Nine .255
The Challenge Ahead .261
Our Equation for Personal Growth .262
How's Your Current Workplace? .265
What is Work? .269

Acknowledgements

No book is complete without some heartfelt words of acknowledgement and ours is no different. As it is with most things in life, the "simple idea" for a book took on a life of its own and, as our passion grew to get it right, it became a three-year writing journey. At various points, both in despair and joy, there were critical people on our path that made a difference.

First, we both acknowledge the many workplaces in which we have directly experienced less than soul-inspiring leadership in action or witnessed others' spirits being crushed before our very eyes. While you might assume some sarcasm, our gratitude is quite genuine, for without an opportunity to live through those situations, how would we have ever developed such excellent "how-not-to" insights?

Not that there have not also been wonderful role models. For both of us, it is perhaps a personal regret to have not enjoyed longer those few rare times of privilege when it just seems to "click" and you have the opportunity to do great work with a team you love under the leadership of an intuitive leader. You all know who you are, for many of you remain in one or both of our lives as friends, colleagues, mentors—and sometimes, even references!

Each of us would also like to thank our many clients who over the years have honoured us by taking our counsel and doing great things with it. The gifts we have would not be as great as they are without the continual dialogue we engage in with those trying to make a difference in the world. Often, the only satisfaction you can take as a consultant or speaker is to hold onto the fact that you make a difference for your clients; your continual reassurances on this point help our spirits continue to thrive and grow. We are always grateful for your support.

So, despite reservations over what has sometimes shown up in our long careers, there are still many people in our lives worthy of explicit thanks. What follows are deeply personal and heartfelt words of acknowledgement from each of us.

CAROL-ANN HAMILTON

I turn first to my very supportive co-author, James Norrie, who has truly stood by me through thick and thin. If you could picture the uncharitable ways in which I greeted his arrival at a former workplace, you would find it absolutely remarkable for us to be writing this book together, let alone that we have become lifelong friends! Such a positive outcome is purely a testament to James' tenacity in not allowing his former colleague's petty behaviour to downgrade his own personal integrity. Certainly, I had nothing to do with it at the time! Undaunted, James ushered me into a new workplace when my level of discouragement could not have been lower and it was he (along with other tremendous colleagues of ours) with whom I dined the night of our termination from that same employer.

Always, always, *always*, James begins conversations through endorsement and acknowledgement of what might be going on in others' lives before sharing his own—sometimes, I think to his detriment, for his selflessness invites others to nourish themselves on his kindness while easily forgetting he, too, may be experiencing woes. In the face of his constant humour, grace under pressure, great thoughtfulness, enormous intelligence, commitment to learning and expansive spirit, I bow with utmost honour.

To my growing circles of friends and colleagues, I offer my heartfelt awe and wonder for the marvelous 'mirrors' they are proving to be in my life. Their understanding of who I really am at the core continues to astound me. Through their encouragement, I have come to trust the wisdom of my words and to realize the value of what I have to communicate. They so often tell me, *"The world needs you, Carol-Ann."* For this, I want to weep with gratitude. It would almost be a sign of disrespect not to listen to their counsel.

To my parents, Bill and Anne, I cannot begin to express enough my appreciation for all they have done for me throughout my life, and for all they continue to do. Only now do I even begin to become aware of all they have sacrificed for me. Without a doubt, the best gift of all has been our conversations in recent years, during which we have truly come to 'know' one another as adults. Thank you, Mom and Dad.

And to Derek, my dear husband, life partner and best friend of the past twenty years, I owe the greatest acknowledgement of all. Although I remember vigorously railing against his early suggestions to not put "all my eggs in his basket" while we discussed marriage, I now continuously delight in this very quality of freedom he brings to our relationship. You see, I believe his wise self knew it would simply not be smart to stand in the way of his wife once she came fully into her life purpose! In order to do my work in the world, I need much latitude. Derek offers this to me, all the while remaining the steadying and reassuring platform from which I am able to travel into uncharted realms as a pioneer-visionary. Perhaps I would still be doing this work without him in my life, but trust me, it would be a very different life indeed. Derek, you know you mean the world to me and I delight in our having crossed paths. Thank you for truly 'seeing' me in my essence and for taking every opportunity to champion me. I love you with all my heart.

P.S. *Derek would be very annoyed if I did not thank our cats, Boogy and Impy, for their contributions to this book which have been in the form of walking across the keyboard while I am trying to compose and lying spread-eagled across pages of manuscript while I try in vain to edit my words.*

JAMES NORRIE

There have been times of great joy in my life and times of great sadness. I have known the unbridled optimism of youth extinguished by the wrenching arrival of adulthood. The high points have seemed to offer endless vistas of new opportunities, while the lows have inflicted harm and pain that was almost unendurable. Yet, what would life be without the ability to feel?

It's taken me this many years to become a "whole spirit," and only now do I feel like I am coming into my own with an ability to truly make my life's purpose a reality. In this process, you come to realize the impact that others have had on you, and as you mature, you become even more grateful for their role in your lives. For me, one of the greatest gifts was the arrival into my life of my two daughters, Lia and Jillian. It is through their constant presence and unconditional love that I am reminded every day of what a privilege it is to be their dad. Both their mother and I are very proud of them and wait with anticipation to see what their own futures will hold for them and for us.

To my mom and dad, I offer a special acknowledgement for all that they have already done and anticipate with joy that which is still left for them to do. I am grateful for their love and support and also for that of my brother (but he must know that already!), my sister, and their respective families.

The voices of my many friends, both near and far away, remain strong in my heart and mind—encouraging much of what many of them will come to see as their direct contributions to this book. I remain eternally grateful that, of all the constants in my life, good friends are among the most important and I am blessed to have you all. These range from childhood friends to the close camaraderie of a gaggle of university friends and others I have been lucky enough to get to know more recently. Partial lists are a problem, full lists are a risk, and so you will all just have to be secure enough to know you are included (albeit silently) herein!

It goes without saying that one's partner in life is always worth waiting for and that the journey is always better with them along. You are a very special person and you have much to offer the world and I'm glad you're always there for me.

As with any endeavour, you are only as good as the team you work with and none is more important to the team that produced this book than Carol-Ann Hamilton. Along the way we have laughed and cried, but we have created an excellent book and the entire credit for this, from the original idea to its timely completion, is yours. You are a wonder to watch; you have wisdom galore, and I absolutely love working with you! But this is only the beginning and we have lots left to do before we are done!

So, without further ado and with no further acknowledgements, we both offer you our best hopes that this book will—in some small but important way—touch you at your soul's core and begin to make a difference in your life.

Preface

Writing this book has been a journey and an adventure. In the three years since the first granule of an idea implanted itself into our minds, a varied collection of seeds has sprouted in our personal, work and societal 'gardens.' Some of the blossoming was anticipated, but much of what germinated was an unexpected harvest. Certainly, it has been bountiful—in more ways than one!

In that short time, we have been terminated on the same day from a shared workplace, one of us has switched careers, one of us joined a workplace that marked a new professional direction and both of us have attempted to keep alive our real work in the world. In the meantime, the world changed forever on September 11, 2001. Hardly would we have imagined, while brainstorming book possibilities in December 1999, that such a galvanizing force would cross humanity's path a mere twenty-one months later. Never will things be quite the same, and yet they have changed very little.

We continue with regularity to receive emails like:

> *You know you work in corporate America if... you sat at the same desk for four years and worked for three different companies... you learn about your layoff on CNN... salaries of Executive Board members are higher than all the Third World countries' annual budgets combined... it's dark when you drive to and from work... free food left over from meetings is your main staple... Dilbert cartoons hang outside every cubicle and are read by your co-workers only... and vacation is something you roll over to next year.*

These messages would otherwise be downright demoralizing were it not equally true that we live in a profoundly transformational time. We sense an insatiable hunger for meaning and purposefulness from everywhere in the world. In the closing days of 2001, never did so many ask such fundamental human questions about who they are and why they are here. To this day, we quibble with the form of this awakening, but if the net result is that people finally pause and reflect upon what is really important in life, then so be it.

Whether on a global, national or individual scale—hearts everywhere are yearning for spiritual renewal. On a professional level, too, the burning issue of spirituality is soaring its way to the top of business agendas. No more are employees prepared to function as mere cogs in the organizational wheel. Indeed, they expect their employers to engage their souls through inspirational visions that rouse their heartfelt desire to contribute to a higher cause.

Yet, in numerous people's experience, organizational life has largely ceased to be a source of inspiration and joy. Consider this: how many of North America's 100-plus million workers can truly say they are fulfilled? Sadly, most of us seldom think of our work as a vital means of soul-expression. But it should stir deep desires for service, growth and appreciation by offering an essential outlet for our innermost quest for nourishment of the whole person.

Certainly, our message is perfectly timed to tap into keen and widespread interest in practical solutions to the burgeoning dilemma of how organizations can embrace employees' spiritual aspirations. Audiences from senior executives in Fortune 500 firms looking to make their mark on company culture to budding entrepreneurs looking to find the right 'formula' to build their businesses will find information of value. Aging "Baby Boomers," now beginning to seek more than simple material success, will resonate with thought-provoking content about leaving a lasting legacy in all they do, including work. "Generation X-ers" who may have initially opted out of the traditional job market will experience restored faith that there is a way to join the mainstream and still exercise their personal mission to achieve fulfilling working lives.

We offer with deepest respect, in answer to this universal cry to transform the workplace, *The A to Z Guide to Soul-Inspiring Leadership*. It is our hope that this how-to book will become your definitive guide on reincorporating soul and spirit into the workplace. By sharing anecdotes and illustrations from our years of experience in the business world, combined with a host of practical resources, we aim to help you express your own true purpose and vision. Written to be highly accessible, we tried to make a complex topic deceptively simple. May it serve as your personal blueprint to success!

By moving out of the purely inspirational realm into a focus on implementing proven ideas in real workplaces, we are appealing to all who recognize that past-century thinking will not work in the new economy. The days of "business as usual" are over. Blasted with the impetus to continuously reinvent, companies will increasingly need adaptable knowledge workers, able to think and act outside the box. How better, we assert, to encourage this kind of contribution than through the core leadership principles that guide our thinking:

"How things *really* are around here" starts with leadership. Like it or not, character and values flow from the top of the 'house' and they tell people plenty about what the organization actually stands for.

Personal leadership lies at the very core of effectively leading others. We challenge you toward inner transformation.

Leaders are 'servants' to their employees. We call upon leaders to daily care for the soul by putting people first through heartfelt appreciation for their inherent value and uniqueness.

Conversely, one must never underestimate the grave consequences of allowing our workplaces to erode the human spirit. The destructive effects of miserable morale, intimidated employees and other spiritual deficiencies can be read in decreased productivity, skyrocketing health-care costs and double-digit turnover as people exit to more congenial settings. Improving how people work together will become a critical performance lever as organizations begin to realize that investment in employees' overall wellness creates a more resilient and focused workplace, able to prosper in a competitive global environment.

While the imperative to build soul-inspiring environments may have stemmed from marketplace demands, we look forward to the day when organizations will genuinely believe it is simply the right thing to do. Spirituality in the workplace is good for business and good for people. Generating outstanding profits and nurturing the human spirit are not mutually exclusive; they are synonymous. In those organizations that already appreciate this truth, loyalty, commitment and high performance naturally ensue from leaders' innate desire to foster the respect and dignity for which their employees so yearn. From them, we draw great hope.

Clearly, we are not so naïve as to assume this unstoppable social revolution will always be an easy journey. Indeed, humanity's transformation to unprecedented levels of "spiritual intelligence" implies for us all unswerving courage as we voyage into territory that has few guideposts. In sharing with you our life's work, we are simply doing our small part toward one day transporting our workplaces to unimagined heights of possibility. In rendering our 'prescription' for business success in the twenty-first century, it is our intention that people need no longer leave their souls at home or at the company gate. Such an envisioned future, we believe, is worth the half of our lives we spend at work!

Acknowledgement

> **There are two things people want more than sex and money—recognition and praise.**
>
> — Mary Kay Ash

Remember how learning to say "*please*" and "*thank you*" were so much a part of your childhood? So why, as we enter adulthood, do we believe these niceties are no longer important? If we look carefully within, we still find that small child beneath the adult veneer. Whether we feel comfortable admitting it or not, we take that child to work each day.

In order to cope, many of us have learned to shield our inner core from attack. We pretend not to need positive "strokes" (i.e., feedback). We put on stoic masks and act as if it doesn't matter that our days are filled with endless constructive criticism about our weaknesses.

What a shame we have come to believe positive feedback

somehow needs to be given in measured doses. It's as if the antiquated "*spare the rod, spoil the child*" belief has crept into our business mindset. Are we thinking people's heads will swell if we congratulate them for a job well done? And even if they do, what are we really afraid of?

Are we concerned it will take too long to fit acknowledgement into already crammed days? If this is so for you, we find it takes no longer than a passing comment or handshake, or visiting people at their workstations. Also, consider a round of feedback during meetings to recognize those who have gone above and beyond. We did these very things in a mutual workplace. Senior leadership meetings began each week by acknowledging members' contributions from other teams, followed up with a card from the President. We can cite countless examples of pleasant surprise when these notes of thanks were hand-delivered to employees. Their faces absolutely lit up in response to our appreciation—proof positive of the lasting impact of kudos.

When you set out to recognize people for their efforts, please do so with an open heart and spirit. Here is a great example of what not to do, which we now refer to as "The Cookie Incident." In this organization, a week-long campaign was launched with the positive intention to provide treats at people's desks each morning. Early on day one, we became aware of hushed yet frenzied activity to ready small cookies for distribution. Why the clandestine conversation, you ask? It turns out only employees were deemed entitled to receive the treats, even though this business unit had many contractors whose workstations were located right next to full-time associates. We think you can picture the consternation over strict instructions to give cookies only to full- and part-time team members (despite the company being able to afford cookies for all). Needless to say, the situation worsened once people arrived at work, resulting in uncomfortable explanations about why some were not getting cookies. This remains a small but important example of how well intentioned acts of acknowledgement can be undone by the insensitivity of corporate execution. What started as a novel idea became overshadowed by senior management's bureaucratic failure to keep their eye on the real ball—the desire to recognize people through thoughtful yet inexpensive gestures.

On a more positive note, consider the powerful impact of unexpected public recognition done well. For eight months, both of us participated in a corporate coaching program; the purpose was to strengthen our personal leadership skills, in part by doing one-on-one coaching with colleagues. Given the intensive nature of the initiative, we were encouraged to invite to our Graduation Day those with whom we had been practicing our skills, for it was their graduation in many ways as well. In sharing our experiences with the audience, we realized how important it was to thank our internal coaching 'clients' for the privilege to work with them in this unique relationship. For example, we remarked that our teammates' openness to learning made the experience highly memorable, resulting in tremendous personal growth for all of us.

Our coachees and others commented afterwards that they were literally shaking in their chairs from the depth of our individual appreciation, delivered in a group setting. We agreed this was a most special occasion—for them, because of the lasting impression such deep praise created in their lives, and for us, because it was more important to use our time onstage to speak about others' greatness than to create personal fanfare around our own learning. This example also bespeaks the humility of soul-inspiring leaders. For them, acknowledgement is selfless and designed to build up the other person. One thinks of Mother Teresa, for example, who never put herself in the spotlight unless it would have served her charges in some way.

As this story further illustrates, feedback must be specific and genuine. Since people can readily spot phony compliments, say nothing at all rather than be insincere. This advice particularly holds true if team members view you as ungenerous in offering positive feedback. Your sudden liberal sharing could otherwise risk becoming a flavour of the month, as in "*Uh-oh, the boss has been to another one of those feedback seminars.*"

When acknowledging others, soul-inspiring leaders not only recognize accomplishments, they spend as much—if not more—time recognizing people for who they are. Rather than see people simply as human "doings," they recognize them as human "beings," valuable for that reason alone. In coaching, we call this skill acknowledging, because it is different from complimenting. Compliments are usually about us, as in, "*I admired your work on that project.*" Instead, acknowledgements start with the word "*you,*" and they speak to the unique talents and qualities the person possesses or brought to bear on an assignment, as in "*You were so dedicated and persevering in the way you brought that project to completion.*" As practitioners of the axiom, "*there is nothing so unequal as the equal treatment of unequals,*" soul-inspiring leaders respond to differences in unique ways that reach each person individually. Kudos to reinforce both team members' individuality and their interactions with others come naturally, willingly and often from those who lead well.

Of course, we are not so idealistic as to imagine we do not ever have to deliver difficult messages about required performance improvements—even in soul-inspiring workplaces. If anything, true leaders are particularly skilled in the art of "tough conversations." Adept at communication, they emphasize voice tone and body language (the *how*) when engaging in these challenging exchanges. They know one can deliver specific feedback (the *what* part of communication, embodied in words), but if it injures another's spirit, negative effects will far outlast any positive behaviour impacts.

Our own understanding of these points has been clarified on a number of occasions when consulting with leaders who repeatedly undermine their valid comments through emotionally damaging interactions. For example, one leader with whom we consulted experienced one hundred percent turnover in her team in less than two years, simply because of the abusive nature of her communication style (back to the *how*) and not because of what she necessarily said. The enormous impact of how acknowledgement is delivered has become so striking for us over the years that we have come to capture it by way of the first of nine "Simple Leadership Equations" you will find herein:

SIMPLE LEADERSHIP EQUATION #1:

Effective Recognition = Content + Context
(the what) *(the how)*

You can deliver a perfectly valid message (the *what*), but if done in such a way as to wound the other person, you must question whether your feedback can be called soul-inspiring at all. On the other hand, a great *how* (the context) can be equally ineffectual if you never get around to delivering the *what* (the conversation about results, or content). You will see equations repeated throughout this book as a way to capture, in a nutshell, core concepts we believe will be striking to our readers. So, stay tuned for more!

In the meantime, let us return to this notion of difficult performance conversations. In these situations, we regularly find ourselves coaching leaders to position performance improvement as an "area of opportunity"—not a punishing exchange, as described in our preceding example. Improvement suggests continuous learning and ongoing opportunities to better one's self toward higher achievement. By eliminating negative connotations of vocabulary such as "constructive criticism," we allow people to hear without becoming defensive, knowing their souls won't be battered in yet another "*let me give you some feedback*" session. Regular dialogue also negates year-end surprises, making the oft-dreaded performance appraisal more effective and efficient.

Now, you might think people should just know how they are doing without your telling them. To a degree, that's true. However, a prime reason most appraisals become such shocking assaults on self-worth is that, rather than giving frequent feedback and supportive coaching along the way, leaders instead save it all until it's too late! Preferring their superstars, they spend time stroking those individuals' already healthy egos and let what they view as the losers fend for themselves. Granted, it is easier to spend time with your cream-of-the-crop players, but that is no reason to let the rest sink or swim. Yet, we see this behaviour all the time in our client organizations. They miss the fact that real performance improvement comes not from the top third, but from the bottom third—the very group that can most use some acknowledgement!

We suggest that challenging employees to open up their full capability represents a wonderful opportunity to apply soul-inspiring leadership practices. How you deal with poor performers makes all the difference between being an employer respected for treating people consistently, fairly and professionally, and one that leaves these important tenets to chance. In fact, one of the psychology theories we use in our practices says humans have such a high need for acknowledgement that they will even seek out negative attention or feedback rather than receive no recognition whatsoever. All the more reason to clearly distinguish poor performance caused by lack of skill versus underlying attitudes that, corrected, could actually produce stellar results. Organizations that truly understand this distinction and the power of positive over negative reinforcement will benefit most from taking action on these points.

Unfortunately, so long as there are training brochures promoting "*Criticism and Discipline Skills For Managers*"—and we get 'em—we are forced to conclude the tough-guy approach to leadership is alive and well. When these workshops become something like "*Giving Sincere and Daily Praise to All Team Members*," we will know acknowledgement is entrenched as a vital, uplifting mechanism for releasing each and every employee's full potential.

QUESTIONS FOR REFLECTION

- When was the last time you said "*please*" or "*thank you*" to someone in your workplace?

- How generous are you in offering positive feedback to colleagues at all levels in your organization?
- Do you believe performance is enhanced by the "carrot," or do you assume extraordinary effort is an inherent part of the job requirements?

DO'S AND DON'TS

- **Do** recognize people for who they are (i.e., their unique talents, gifts and characteristics), using statements that start with "*you.*"
- **Do** emphasize the *how* (voice tone, body language, context, compassion) in your communications, not just the *what* (your actual words).
- **Do** continuously look for creative ways to acknowledge and recognize people (simple, low-effort and inexpensive can have just as much impact as the opposite).
- **Do not** refer to feedback for improvement as constructive criticism aimed at weaknesses; **do** talk about areas of opportunity and how to build on strengths.
- **Do not** express your feedback in vague terms and fail to make it genuine.

EXERCISE FOR TEAM LEARNING

Conduct an experiment for one week where you and your team members actively look only for ways to "catch others doing things right." Have everyone record their observations and people's reactions in journals you buy for you and your team. Get together after one week and discuss your observations as a group. Talk about what people noticed in focusing on what's right rather than what's wrong. Have each person note the learning this exercise elicited for him or her, and how he or she will commit to behaving differently in the future related to acknowledgement.

FIRST STEPS ALONG THE WAY

Assigned Task	Expected Outcome
Allocate set amounts of time and money to institute spontaneous acts of kindness in your workplace. This would involve purchasing an array of small items people would enjoy (food, inspirational tokens, certificates, etc.), and determining the frequency plus means to anonymously hand out these gifts, ultimately including each person on your team.	*Shows appreciation through personalized treats that bring people joy. As these tokens are not intended to acknowledge a job well done, their significance is actually more profound. This is because employees are not used to receiving gifts "out of the blue." When thanks is given out, it is usually for something the person has done, and not "just because I wanted to acknowledge you as a person."*
Revisit your company's Reward & Recognition systems and policies. Investigate for what reasons and how often employees are rewarded and recognized. If you locate imbalances, determine how and when these will be addressed.	*Creates balance between reward and recognition. Many organizations reward performance using a limited set of methods (e.g., money, certificates of accomplishment, gift items), while overlooking the many ways to recognize employees' contributions to teamwork and other organizational values (e.g., cards, verbal praise, bulletin board postings, etc.).*

Assigned Task	Expected Outcome
Obtain reports or other narrative data from Human Resources on exit interviews and/or current turnover statistics. Analyze this data over time to see how much you can reduce resignations due to lack of positive feedback, as a result of implementing new people-acknowledging practices.	*Committing to constantly demonstrating appreciation toward your people sends clear signals about the value of acknowledgement in your organization. Remember—people crave recognition and they seek it out in the workplaces they join.*

Balance

> When you live as if you'll live forever, it becomes too easy to postpone the thing you know that you must do.
>
> — Elisabeth Kuebler Ross

Life is like a pie—we create, from a variety of ingredients, a composition that can be divided into slices. If we alter any one ingredient, the pie becomes different. If we leave out the sweetener, it becomes tart. If we leave out the flour, it may not even be a pie at all. How it tastes is up to us. The recipe influences the outcome—barring an unpredictable oven! And when it's time to serve our salivating guests, they look forward to receiving their slice according to their wishes—some like a thin sliver and others can't wait for the wedge with the whipping cream.

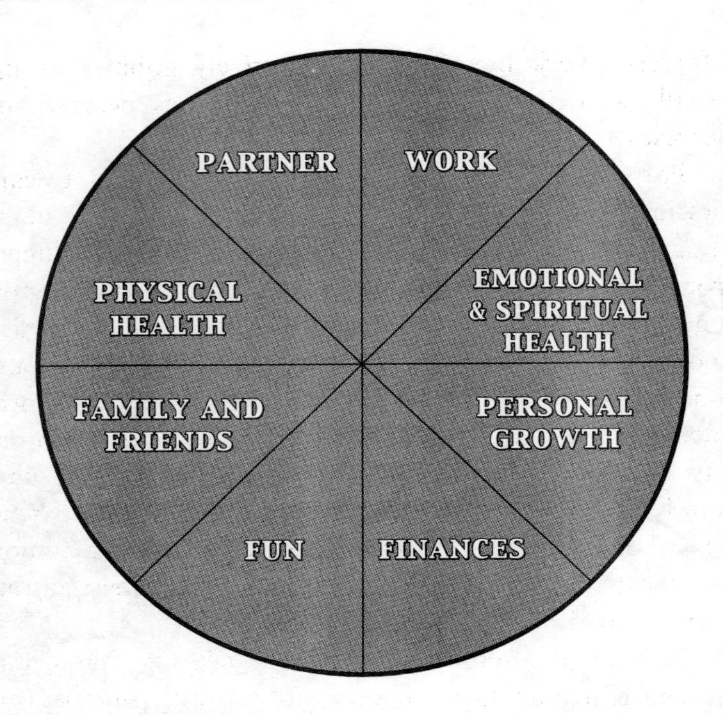

Whatever our preferences, we would hardly consider it fair to give half the pie (or more) to just one person. And we would be somewhat offended if we were anticipating blueberry pie, but our host left out the blueberries. Yet, this is precisely how many of us apportion the 'pie' that is our life. We unconsciously throw together some ingredients, lose track while it bakes and then wonder why we pull a burnt mess from the oven.

While many treat work as the single largest piece, it is but one slice of the total pie. We forget it is equally composed of: relationships (family and friends, partner); health (physical, emotional and spiritual); personal growth; finances; fun. When we allow work to consume us, the remaining sectors are forced to compete for the meagre leftovers. Work literally and figuratively gobbles us up, usually sacrificing those people and things nearest and dearest to our hearts—loved ones and health.

Particularly worrisome is the growing trend toward viewing being busy as a status symbol. We are not talking about being positively busy, defined as deriving fulfillment from dedicating yourself to what you consider most important. We are talking about being driven by and complaining about hectic daily routines, putting off family, friends and other essential priorities until they can be squeezed months later into booked-up calendars—leaving more room in our day for work! With cellphones, buzzers and beepers constantly on, there is almost nowhere on the planet we cannot be reached. On top of it, many people equate their importance with how often they are paged for business during social activities.

Increasingly, for every person stuck on this nerve-wracking treadmill, an equal and growing number are leaving the rat race for greater balance and freedom. They have realized corner offices and large salaries are not worth the failed relationships, grown-up children one does not really know, declining health and soul-sickness. They refuse to arrive at the end of life only to find truth in Peggy Lee's famous rendition of "*Is That All There Is?*" Coming to their senses, they realize work anxiety can poison our entire body's systems, destroying the very vehicle we need to carry out our work in the world. Left unchecked, we succumb to what the Japanese call *karoshi*, or death from overwork.

In one of our former workplaces, a most unusual horror shockingly drove home the point that we never know what lies around the corner, and so must not allow work to eat up our limited time on Earth. Twice in a period of two years, two young employees died suddenly—one at thirty-nine years of age, while checking out of her hotel room on a business trip, and another at twenty-seven years old in a car accident while on a well-deserved vacation. Believe us when we say that tragedies of such magnitude, especially back-to-back, sent us reeling into renewed examination of our own lives. As death is not 'supposed' to happen to young people, we were instantaneously catapulted into introspection concerning what is really important. Viewing these wonderful women's pictures while mourning, writing of their impact in journals given to grief-stricken parents, speaking and crying at their memorial services—what a dramatic wake-up call to realize how precious our lives are. For a few days, work became truly insignificant, while family, friends, health and appreciation of life became everyone's focus.

In sharing these moving examples, we profoundly hope you never have to go through such extreme experiences before taking action to demonstrate that work is but one slice of life's pie. We believe compassionate leaders realize that people cannot be split into fragmented parts—as if they have a business self they bring to work while the remaining self gets shelved, and vice versa. If anything, compassionate leaders strive to accommodate employees' lives so as to minimize conflicts between work and home. While some would say pandering to outside-of-work concerns has no place in the business world, soul-inspiring leaders know that helping people attend to personal matters ultimately results in greater focus on work while at work.

Forward-looking organizations believe the costs of investing in team members' welfare are far outweighed by gains, including reducing the risk of losing top talent to burnout. At a time when many employers are concerned about skyrocketing health-care costs (through escalating Employee Assistance Program expenditures and growing numbers of short-term disability claims that explode into unmanageable long-term disability payouts), it would seem fiscally prudent to take steps to reduce this bottom-line drain. Often still treated as a reactive step, we believe the demand for organizations to minister to balance will increasingly become a non-negotiable proactive business decision to address employee protests against inhumane workplaces.

Human Resources survey data consistently supports our conclusions. Time and again, the most sought-after items in a chosen employer among newly hired professionals are flexible arrangements (including working from home and job-sharing), regular sabbaticals, training, paid time off, casual environments, child- and elder-care assistance, and an emphasis on control over their working lives. To assist those needing to take unscheduled days off to deal with family issues, innovative organizations institute bankable "mental health days." And, to help associates cope with chore-laden lives, many employers now offer on-site services like driver's license renewal, shoe repair, dry cleaning and drugstore delivery. Talk about time savers!

These smart companies realize they gain, in return, a people advantage more valuable than any kind of competitive advantage borne of overusing people and not encouraging balance. Think about the goodwill and loyalty generated by a family policy that offers an employee a promotion while on maternity leave and allows her to create a highly flexible workweek upon her return—because she is so valuable. This true story displays a key quality of people-centric organizations. Viewing work-life balance holistically, they weave it seamlessly into the very fabric of daily operations.

While much to-do has been made about work-life balance programs, our experience consulting with organizations looking to implement these philosophies suggests that, all too often, they are nothing more than phantom programs. While a noted part of policy, in reality they have virtually no real impact on employees' lives. This is because any practice treated as a program quickly risks becoming a program-of-the-month. Balance is not a program one does; it is a way of being one believes in and lives. As such, work-life balance ought to be a core value, tracked and measured as a key performance indicator, as opposed to being motivated by a business desire to look good or by the ulterior motive of increasing profits through healthier employees with a greater capacity to take on more work.

Leaders must exemplify balance as a core value through their own behaviour. Like it or not, your team constantly monitors how much balance you personally demonstrate. If you are a workaholic who puts career ahead of all else and expects the same from your staff, your implicit and explicit messaging will make it exceptionally difficult for those who leave on time to attend to families, personal interests and social engagements.

Soul-inspiring leaders distinguish themselves by pointing out unhealthy behaviour patterns like putting in excessive overtime and regularly taking work home, and they welcome similar feedback. They question those who do not take their full vacations, rather than holding up such individuals as superstars. Whereas in unbalanced organizations, employees who consistently put in twelve-hour days are lauded as heroes, in people-friendly workplaces they are targeted for "work smarter, not harder" campaigns!

Merely being in one's chair each day, or what is called "face time," is unheard-of in leading-edge settings. Face time in no way translates into productivity, as much as untrusting leaders cling to this belief. Their implicit suggestion is: "*Unless I can keep my eyes on you at all times, I cannot trust you are getting the work done.*" These same leaders typically disagree with forward-looking initiatives like telecommuting. However, if number of hours spent at work is the sole measure of your shareholder value, we propose you have a broader systemic issue than simply work-life balance!

In closing, let's circle back to the notion of your life as a pie. While we used this metaphor for illustrative purposes, in reality the pie cannot be quite as neatly divided as we earlier suggested. That is because your life is the whole pie, and therefore work is but one slice. Your task is to find ways to sustain equilibrium within your whole life. Let's try an exercise we often do at workshops we conduct. To lock in this sense of equilibrium, imagine life as a game in which you are juggling five balls—work, family, health, friends and hobbies (or a different set of categories). Striving to keep all of them in the air, you soon realize work is a rubber ball. If you drop it, it bounces back. The other four, made of glass, are scuffed, damaged or shattered if dropped.

In other words, if any of us died tomorrow, the organization would find a way to replace us in a matter of days, whereas the family we left behind would feel the loss for the rest of their lives. Talk about a way to put work into perspective! Progressive employers realize this truth. And that is why soul-inspiring leaders reinforce balance by consistently reminding people that their in-trays will be full when they pass away. They always support going home at the end of the day, as opposed to finishing that one last piece of work. You never know—it might be your last day on Earth.

QUESTIONS FOR REFLECTION

- How much of your sense of self is tied up with doing and achieving at work?
- Would your friends and family say you spend enough time with them? Why or why not?
- What messages does your behaviour communicate to people about the degree to which you value work-life balance?

DO'S AND DON'TS

- **Do** remember work is only one aspect of your whole life.
- **Do** examine whether balance is universally available to everyone in your workplace.
- **Do** "get with the program" by proactively instituting the kinds of flexible, people-centric practices leading-edge employers use to attract and retain high-potential performers.
- **Do not** treat balance as a 'program' one 'does.'
- **Do not** measure productivity or contribution using "face time" as your indicator.

EXERCISE FOR TEAM LEARNING

Use a team meeting to have each person draw a 'pie' divided according to the percentages they feel your workplace emphasizes these elements: career; health (emotional and spiritual); relationships (friends, family, partner); personal growth; fun; environment (physical). Have each person individually comment on the extent to which they would say your organization is balanced or imbalanced. Discuss as a team what change(s) people would recommend to help make your environment more balanced. Bring those proposals to your next leadership team meeting. Ask for volunteers to help you implement the accepted recommendations and keep following up with your team on actions taken.

FIRST STEPS ALONG THE WAY

Assigned Task	*Expected Outcome*
Display and circulate materials about wellness in prominent locations in your workplace. Partner with your providers to schedule special workshops and circulate information about work-life balance, stress management and related topics.	*Employees will know you place importance on living a balanced life. By your investment in these interventions, people will realize you are not just giving lip service, and you earnestly wish to improve the quality of their working lives.*

Assigned Task	Expected Outcome
Encourage people to extend their calendaring systems to a whole-life approach. This means making sure to schedule important personal events, and not just work priorities. If value-added, consider sending employees to training providers that help people schedule their lives according to these values-based philosophies.	*Creates alignment across the organization in how people schedule their work-home lives. Reduces work-home conflicts. Regularly encouraging your team members to keep each other 'honest' about their outside-of-work commitments reinforces your intention to reward balanced behaviour.*

Courage

> **The reasonable man adapts himself to the conditions that surround him. The unreasonable man adapts the surrounding conditions to himself. All progress depends on the unreasonable man.**
>
> **—George Bernard Shaw**

What is courage? How do you know if you have it? If you have it, how do you consistently demonstrate it to others? While seemingly hard to define, we actually have an operating definition of courage that we use with our clients: *Courage is a selfless act to do what is right regardless of personal consequences.*

Now, in calling for courage, we are aware that this can be confused with "whistle blowing" and other behaviours, many of which have been highlighted during recent corporate scandals (Enron, Tyco, Worldcom and others). It is clear that in these instances, courage is *essential* and must be practiced by those not wishing to sacrifice their own integrity to the corporate demons within. This is a very real and significant issue.

But courage does not always suggest "going public," especially if this is done more in self-interest than in the company's best interests. This is a very fine line and one that each of you could be called upon to make decisions about at some point in your career.

When we talk about courage, we mean the ability to suspend self-interest and *do what's right*. Sounds easy, doesn't it? Well, it is not. What if it called for a vice-president to merge her function with another and then offer to lay herself off as redundant? Would she have the courage to do what was right and make a choice that potentially had negative personal consequences? Or how about the executive called upon to close a money-losing division because of short-term budget pressure when he knows for a fact the division could improve dramatically if given a long-term chance to succeed—what should he do and why? Or what about ignoring the prevailing legal wisdom of never admitting responsibility for anything and instead concluding the company was liable for something and should pay as a consequence? What would you do?

These are the sorts of business, legal and moral dilemmas that occur every day in corporations all over the world, and they are the essence of courage. What will you do when you find yourself in this kind of position? Will you do what is right, or will you do what is prescribed, recommended or assumed as the right thing?

The two are rarely the same. If you want extraordinary results, you must consistently take a courageous stand for what is right. You cannot choose to be courageous when it is convenient and then abandon this principle when it is not. People watch you make the ordinary, mundane decisions of everyday work as much as they watch you make the extraordinary, high impact decisions.

Regrettably, many employees' experience of leadership is spineless. In these suspect organizations, the question of the day is: "*How little courage can we get away with?*" At the time of writing, our press is littered with the debris of outrageous liars being ejected from the tops of corporate monoliths. These raiders of the proverbial cookie jar seemingly had no compulsion to follow their conscience while planning their heists, but are now self-righteously indignant about getting caught. As one headline attested, "*It's time to restructure our corporate culture.*" The authors of this business ethics column wrote that we must completely rethink and restructure how the corporate environment operates so as to ultimately prevent such individuals from ever getting near the CEO's chair. We could not agree more! It is a central tenet in our goal to transform the workplace to one of courage and truth-telling.

In our vision, soul-inspiring leaders leave no doubt that they possess the courage of their convictions. They tell it like it is. The buck stops with them. Their word is sacred and their integrity uncompromising. They do not waver when the going gets tough; they stay the course. Soul-inspiring leaders are trusted and trustworthy.

In courageous organizations, leaders step out from behind the insulation of their inner circle to deal with real issues that real people face on the front lines. When difficult messages have to be delivered, they go eyeball-to-eyeball with their workforce, taking the heat of controversy in response to pressing questions. They do not let "spin doctors" rob them of their integrity. Unlike the milquetoasts of the business world who refuse to face reality by keeping their ostrich-heads firmly planted in the sand, courageous leaders value blunt honesty—always. They know people's level of trust in leadership is reflected in their trust in words, together with a reliance on action and follow-through. Rather than dodge 'bullets' by hiding behind e-mails, they stand up to so-called hard-nosed employees. Soul-inspiring leaders speak the truth for the meek and silent.

Where truth-tellers—because they refuse to be molded by constricted expectations—are labeled by many organizations as "problem employees" who need "corrective measures," brave leaders foster living according to inner truth. They seek out those who refuse to sidestep what needs to be said. They constantly urge employees to fearlessly point out "*the emperor is wearing no clothes*." They know withholding serves no one. They believe a real relationship is not about being nice; it is founded on being real. When soul-inspiring leaders demonstrate the will to invite truth-telling, employees gain a wonderful model of the art of being direct in the best sense.

One company with whom we consulted refers to this competency as managerial courage—a term capturing the essence of the leader with conviction. This is the leader who is willing to take tough stands on behalf of his or her team, even when these viewpoints are unpopular with peers. Soul-inspiring leaders are not afraid to make themselves somewhat dangerous in the world, if this is what it takes to ensure issues are not swept under the carpet.

When people perceive their leaders as having this kind of credibility, they often feel a stronger sense of team spirit and commitment. Conversely, when people perceive leaders as weak, they are more apt to feel unsupported and privately (if not publicly) criticize the employer. Factors that would not normally be prime motivators, such as money, become a focus. Our own careers support this pattern. When reporting to people we did not respect, our performance was more often than not strictly based on professionalism rather than desire, whereas credible leaders encouraged us to shine, making us want to help them be successful in the process.

As you contemplate how you will be perceived as a courageous leader in your workplace, take with you this story about the business impact of a weak-kneed organization's refusal to courageously stay the course through challenging times. Its basis is derived from our consultation with senior management in the development of a new business unit. Initially we were endorsed for generating a fresh vision unconfined by existing corporate practices. The senior team applauded our innovative approaches, for they attracted a surprising number of long-term team members to uproot their lives and move into this dynamic environment. Slowly, the parent company began to drag its heels in shifting to a new operating model, causing progress to grind to a painful halt. What was a beacon of hope slowly became a faint glimmer of light fogged over by political power struggles. The passion underlying our motto, "*the way things really are around here*," became a ridiculed scapegoat.

Ultimately, senior leadership lacked the courage to see through their original commitment, preferring to backslide to a more comfortable but stale existence. The costs were steep. Those hired to bring the new culture into being left in droves, causing capability gaps as those left behind lacked the skills to rebuild the organization. Enormous technology and other investments failed to realize projected returns. This company truly became a no-man's land, neither completely retrenched into an old way of being, nor having boldly stepped into an exciting future.

To this day we are left wondering what might have happened had the firm's leadership retained the courage of their earlier convictions. In our view, the time to hold on is precisely when things go awry and the dream appears to be slipping from grasp. The time to stand firm is when it would be far easier to say: "*Who were we kidding? This is the way it's always been and is the way it will always* be. *Who were we to think we could be any different?*" The time to be unreasonable is when people all around you are abandoning hope. When everything hangs in the balance, leaders can either teeter into mediocrity, or they can choose to renew their dedication, drawing recharged conviction from a place deep within their souls. Had this company's leaders stayed the course, we are convinced they would have fulfilled every promise embedded within their new corporate direction.

At the end of the day, no one is saying leading through conviction is easy. However, courage is not the absence of fear; it is proceeding in spite of it. Courage refers to ongoing acts of valour, such as deciding not to hold back something that needs to be said. It is being candid when it may feel perilous. It is facing and hearing others' truths, no matter how uncomfortable. Instead of falling prey to the "chop and change" mentality (as one executive we worked with called it), soul-inspiring leadership is unwavering in its dedication to see through a bold course of action. It is rather like the story of a group of friends traveling across the Irish countryside who came to a formidably high orchard wall and who tossed their hats over the barrier so they would have no choice but to follow them if their voyage was to continue. To be sure, courageous leadership is not for the fainthearted. But then again, how can you expect to be a sheep and yet lead the pack?

QUESTIONS FOR REFLECTION

- To what degree do you invite truth-telling around you and what truths are you most comfortable hearing?
- What do you observe about your own reactions to the truth-tellers on your team, as opposed to those who hold back their opinions?
- How can you incorporate the attributes of the most trustworthy and integrity-based person in your workplace into your own habits?

DO'S AND DON'TS

- **Do** stay the course through challenging times (and if you decide to "fold your cards" rather than "hold" them, do it consciously).
- **Do** remember that people observe your handling of both ordinary, mundane decisions and extraordinary, high-impact ones.
- **Do not** shoot the messenger.
- **Do not** hide behind the 'insulation' by avoiding dealing with people face to face.

EXERCISE FOR TEAM LEARNING

For two weeks, notice how the act of speaking your truth lands with others. By "lands," we mean their verbal and non-verbal reactions to your words and how you say them. Jot notes to yourself in your Learning Journal throughout the process. What are your conclusions? Are certain truths received more easily, with some people more so than with others? To determine what modifications you would make in your truth-telling, follow up by asking colleagues directly for their feedback. In your next team meeting, review your action plan for inviting more truth-telling. Invite team members' ideas for how you can be more truthful with each other (i.e., what behaviours would be demonstrated, what support people need). Draw up a Team Truth-Telling Rules of Engagement, and hold one another accountable for living up to it by telling the truth when someone is not fulfilling these commitments.

FIRST STEPS ALONG THE WAY

Assigned Task	*Expected Outcome*
Institute "truth cards" at the end of company meetings. Use two colours of index cards, one for observations and one for questions. Hand them out so people can anonymously record their comments, collect and shuffle the cards, and then distribute them to a panel of leaders who take turns responding publicly to the items.	*Creates safety and anonymity for those who would otherwise be fearful of expressing their true feelings in a large group setting. Chances are, each "truth card" speaks on behalf of a number of those assembled, providing everyone an opportunity to have their shared unspoken concerns addressed.*

Do an organizational truth-telling audit. Take into your next leadership meeting such questions as: how much truth-telling is encouraged in your organization, which truths are allowable and whether truth-tellers are rewarded or punished. Examine with peers both your formal and informal practices. Develop and communicate specific actions for generating greater 'freedom of speech' across the organization.

Communicating this audit is underway and sharing results with all employees says leaders are serious about wanting to hear the truth from their workforce. Inviting a cross-section of employees to validate the assessment results reinforces that people's opinions count.

Together with the senior leadership team, examine a critical upcoming decision that will require courage of your convictions. Identify points where it would be easy to throw in the towel and develop contingency plans on how you will stay the course through to successful implementation.

Demonstrates proactivity in dealing with those inevitable times when it would be tempting to back down from a difficult course of action. Sharing this thinking with others results in trust and respect for leaders' preparedness to be gutsy, and it encourages everyone to help solve problems as they arise.

Diversity

> **Whenever two people meet there are really six present. There is each man as he sees himself, each as the other person sees him, and each as he really is.**
>
> **—William James**

The age of the generalist and specialist has come and gone—we have clearly evolved into the age of the individualist. That there should be any debate about this point continues to astound us, for the evidence is everywhere. This social trend began with the "Me" generation and has accelerated as we moved into the demographic cohort often referred to as "Generation X." Each successive generation defines itself in its own way and integrates into existing cultural norms on its own terms. However, of interest of us is this general notion of moving from social integration to social isolation. People are increasingly defining themselves as individuals willing to fight against inclusion into any particular group.

To help illustrate this fundamental shift, we need only look to the world of dating. For generations, social institutions like church, social clubs, community centres and even work provided ample opportunity for people to connect and form social relationships. In turn, these often became romances. There was little in the way of dating colleagues—in fact, many entered the workforce on the assumption that they would marry and then perhaps even leave to make a home. This model lasted well over a century.

Social trends today inhibit this 'traditional' model. For instance, we live in a world where it is not "politically correct" to mix the worlds of work and dating. Fewer of us regularly participate in socially-based institutions like churches or community groups, and a general sense of isolation has become part of the modern urban landscape. Thousands of people live side by side in ever-increasing density, but with ever fewer connections to each other. These days, many families are headed by a single parent or are constructed from blended families created by divorce or other non-traditional or unusual family units. Our generally accepted definition of family is now a constantly moving target as, rightfully, those who do not share the traditional definition fight for acceptance and validation. In some societies, the very institution of marriage is being challenged as the preferred choice and the percentage of those remaining outside of this model is increasing.

These trends imply enormous shifts in the world of work, as well. No longer will the next generation of workers feel, think or behave in the same way as the previous one. Companies employing hundreds or thousands of workers will particularly find that their workforce spans several generations. If we accept as typical a working lifespan lasting thirty to forty years for each of us—a realistic expectation today—many organizations could conceivably have two to three generations on their payroll at any given time.

In days gone by, with a fairly homogenous workforce to draw from and an expectation of conformity, managing people was not a significant challenge. In fact, the mere expectation of conformity gave management a certain comfort in its ability to set expectations uniformly, with little risk of interlopers "upsetting the balance." However, as the war for talent heats up and it becomes impossible to meet labour demands without being an employer of choice, the ability to embrace diversity and make it a strength becomes a competitive imperative.

No longer will diversity programs be mere showpieces of human resources departments in order to win awards and praise from others. Instead, diversity will become embedded into the very essence of organizational culture. In soul-inspiring workplaces, people will be engaged at all levels. They will be allowed to contribute their diverse skills and attitudes, molding and shaping the outcome into high-performing, competition-crushing teams. In soul-inspiring organizations, diversity will be a strength to rely upon rather than a problem to manage or contain. Leaders in these workplaces will understand the unique balance that can be achieved when old and young are intertwined, when ethnicity and religion are embraced as qualities that create a truly global company. This is when the age of the individualist will give rise to a culture of tolerance that encourages contribution rather than conformity. And it is in these workplaces that individualists will choose to work.

An interesting example of this would be a friend of ours who is literally a world-famous graphic designer. Trained in his craft and applying his incredible artistic flair, he has created some of the world's best-known corporate logos. Braydon is also an individualist in every sense of the word, crafting a very pleasing life for himself, his partner Jason, a bevy of exotic pets and a townhouse that would knock your socks off. Evenings spent with Braydon and Jason are a joy because of their vibrant spirits.

Working at a large firm, our friend had a very supportive boss who was, after a period of time, promoted and moved to New York. The inbound executive coming to head the Canadian operations was a little older and had been raised as a Baptist in the southern United States. Gordon had been with the company for some time and it was generally assumed that he was an equally capable leader. Shortly after arriving, Gordon decided to invite each of his key staff and their spouses to dinner as a "get-to-know-ya" exercise—absolutely the appropriate thing to do.

Braydon didn't think anything of the invitation and invited Jason to join him. Arriving at the restaurant first, they took their seats and waited for Gordon to arrive. As they chatted about their days, Gordon arrived at the table and greeted Braydon warmly. "*Nice to see you,*" he said."*I'm so glad you were able to bring along a friend to keep you company.*" A look of shock crossed Braydon's face. Thunderclouds passed over Jason's head. The tension was rising faster than a thermometer in a desert heat. Braydon moved into recovery: "*Gordon, this is my partner Jason.*"

There was a momentary frown as Gordon processed this information. In that instant, he was making a leadership choice—not one that he was as aware of as he should have been, but a choice nonetheless. Would his personal views interfere with his responsibilities to create a welcoming atmosphere for a key contributor on his team?

The dinner, as it turned out, did not go especially well. Braydon increasingly felt like he could no longer be himself within the firm because of Gordon's pronounced ambivalence about him. While his work was outstanding and his account management skills were second to none, that was not enough—because he was different.

Later that spring, Braydon received an offer from a competing firm. He had often had offers from this firm and many others in fact. But his loyalty to and satisfaction with his current firm had caused him to reject them outright. Not anymore. Within four weeks of that phone call, Braydon was a newly minted vice-president at a competitor. Over the next six months, more than seventy-five percent of his clientele followed him to this new firm, representing total billings in the millions of dollars. Gordon was furious, and told everyone who would listen about *"disloyalty and professional integrity,"* in veiled references to Braydon.

Braydon did not say anything. He did not need to, for his point of view was clear: *"everyone is entitled to his or her own opinion and to being an individual; however, if your point of view comes into conflict with my essence, I owe you nothing."* In his world, something primary had been taken away by a company leader. Braydon no longer felt valued and accepted. Nothing could overcome the isolation he felt only because of who he was.

This story could be repeated millions of times—it happens every day in our world of work. There is a real cost for any leader who does not intrinsically embrace this important point: all people deserve to be accepted for who they are!

Let us hasten to add, we are not suggesting that diversity be perverted to the point of anarchy. It is not our intent to imply effective workplaces—soul-inspiring or otherwise—should be unstructured or lacking in discipline. Nor is this a nod in the direction of some high-tech workplaces with their assorted collections of "free space" thinking rooms, pool tables, dartboards and refrigerators full of high-caffeine colas and snacks (although we should point out we are not against these, either!). Those elements relate more to the overall environment, not to diversity as we represent it here.

Diversity for us is a deeper concept, related to freedom of expression that ensures a sense of congruence between who people truly are and where they choose to work—along with the organization's ability to recruit and retain the best employees for the work to be done. This theme emerges repeatedly in our book, because we feel strongly that leaders who grasp it fundamentally in their own souls will be able to transfer their knowledge into creating soul-inspiring workplaces.

In a similar vein, we want to address those who struggle with the attitude of younger generations, for their views can be dramatically different from those held dear by many senior leaders in organizations today. This dissonance has created a chasm of misunderstanding we refer to as the "goof gap"—that unsuspecting divide between the intentions behind leaders' decisions and how they communicate them versus how the message is received and understood by new generations of workers. Gordon's responses and language in our previous story are good examples of falling into the "goof gap." He should have made it his business to find out about Braydon and deal with any discomfort long before the dinner invitation.

Unwittingly, many otherwise talented leaders with whom we consult have made what they consider good decisions only to find, as they are announced, that more of their credibility has actually evaporated. This occurs because different generations do not share the same values, opinions or expectations about work.

An extreme example of this phenomenon is represented in one of our favourite syndicated cartoons, Dilbert. Many leaders can identify with this behaviour when they are confronted with it humorously over morning coffee, yet they will vigorously deny exhibiting any similar traits when they arrive at the office. Leaders must recognize they are not infallible, and therefore need to embrace diversity of opinion from a range of workers before making decisions.

In so doing, they will profoundly understand the difference between what we call "shelfware" and "selfware." Whereas "selfware" is new programming you install in your inner self that genuinely guides you to new ways of thinking and behaving, "shelfware" remains just that. Diversity may seem to be a hallmark of your leadership style, but if it is relegated to programs on the "shelf" and not evident in your behaviour (but only in your words), then you cannot truly be said to have embraced diversity. On the other hand, if you have spent energy and time reflecting upon your own beliefs about diversity and eliminating biases or prejudices, you have successfully moved in the direction of adjusting your "selfware."

A good example of the need to re-evaluate both these elements is the notion of career pathing. Many companies rushed to herald it as a be-all and end-all for workers who had come to expect a steady stream of promotions over time as evidence of climbing the corporate ladder. Then, in the next wave of consultant-driven corporate reinvention, we re-engineered and process-improved ourselves to the point where we were no longer prepared to sustain multiple layers of positions, often created mostly to satisfy the needs of the workforce. Upon hiring the next few waves, we replaced vertical with horizontal movement; "cross-training" and "skills development" became buzzwords used to placate the workforce as promotions slowed and we discouraged expectations concerning what we had created in the first place! Yet, corporate leaders and human resources professionals drew comfort in their ability to manage these groups as cohorts, groups moving through the system together with similar needs.

More recent generations, upon entering the workplace, have made it clear they want nothing to do with career paths and promotions, but instead want freedom and flexibility to pursue work as, at most, a component of their lives. It should be clear their individual needs cannot be addressed succinctly by any typical career planning program—which has left many of our client companies lost about what to do. In looking around at companies today, we see evidence of this drift everywhere as past tools of the trade begin to lose their effectiveness. Yet, they persist in trying and wind up falling still further into the "goof gap." Program after program is designed to address this group's needs, but totally misses the point that presenting them as *programs* is the issue!

The "goof gap" also arises when a savvy part of the organization on the leading edge of this problem—perhaps recruitment—catches on and tries to help their leaders think differently about it. Yet, they cannot speak or act authoritatively, because managers treat new initiatives that threaten their way of thinking as "shelfware" versus "self-ware." Someone speaks, no one listens and nothing changes. Cynicism sets in.

SIMPLE LEADERSHIP EQUATION #2:

Diversity of Needs = Diversity of Response

This simple secret—our second Simple Leadership Equation—has worked for both of us. A diversity of needs can only be met by an equal diversity of response. The workplace of the future will have to learn to engage its front-line leaders in real leadership by creating organizational responses that meet individual needs rather than enforcing policy or practice, as is often the case today. This fundamental shift is of seismic proportions and overwhelming complexity to implement. However, it also offers an undeniable advantage and tremendous returns that make diversity of thinking a key feature of competitive soul-inspiring environments of the future.

QUESTIONS FOR REFLECTION

- Think about a time when you fell into the "goof gap;" what will you do differently in the future to avoid this problem?
- Is the concept of embracing diversity and individualism a hallmark of your leadership style and practices (selfware), or a hallmark of your words but not behaviour (shelfware)?
- How can you design a diversity-related intervention that uses the concept of "selfware" to embed one powerful change in behaviour that will be obvious to everyone in your organization?

DO'S AND DON'TS

- **Do** think of diversity as freedom of expression/alignment between who people are and where they choose to work.
- **Do** meet diversity of needs with a diversity of response by remembering each person in a given cohort has unique needs.
- **Do not** tumble into the "goof gap"—that chasm between your intentions and how they are communicated versus how they are received and understood by your workforce.
- **Do not** fall prey to the trap of "one size fits all" programs like career paths.

EXERCISE FOR TEAM LEARNING

Locate a corporate program you are either responsible for or with which you have been closely involved. Meet with your leadership team or the group you lead and, referring to this chapter, try to identify how you can begin the process of installing new "selfware" around the diversity concept. Make it safe for people to bring up their biases (i.e., safe to be honest without recrimination), so they can be cleared out of the way. Ask others for their help, both during this conversation and on an ongoing basis, as you work to implement what you have learned.

FIRST STEPS ALONG THE WAY

Assigned Task	*Expected Outcome*
Explore the ethnic diversity of the town or city you live in. Visit neighbourhoods, shops and restaurants you are unfamiliar with. Read about and visit new cultures, trying to understand how cultural traits influence thinking.	*Encourages the beginning of a new awareness of the impact of diversity on thinking and behaviour—both your own and others'.*
Think about where you live and the variety of people in your community. Consider race, religion, gender, age, sexual orientation, level of education and other factors. Would they all feel welcome in your organization? If not, why not? Can you afford to alienate anybody's potential contribution to your success?	*Reflecting on diversity in practical terms helps you recognize potential barriers to those who are "different" than you.*

Emotions

> **We lead by being human. We do not lead by being corporate, professional or institutional.**
>
> **—Paul G. Hawken**

In the Western world, we are at best ambivalent about our feelings. If we even acknowledge their existence, we feel compelled to reconcile our feelings about having feelings by classifying them as either good or bad, OK or not OK. Allowed or forbidden. So-called good feelings are permissible to an extent, but we confine when and how positive emotions are expressed. For many leaders, "*happy, happy, happy!*" is all they want to hear; do not bring them any bad news. Often, anger and sadness are strictly off limits. Certainly, I can recall being labeled as too passionate by leaders uncomfortable with authentic emotional expression—simply because I dared verbalize disagreement rather than squash feelings like my teammates.

One question we therefore pose is: how can we create workplaces where no feeling is good or bad, but just *is*? We are human beings, and to shut off the valve to our emotions is to eliminate some portion of our humanity. Having feelings is perfectly natural. Contrary to the tired advice, "*employees must learn to manage* (also known as *control* and *squelch*) *their emotions*," why not instead teach them to deal with issues openly and directly? Bringing out pent-up emotions purges festering resentment, heals unhealthy relationships and releases blocked creativity.

Of course, we acknowledge that how we deal with feelings makes all the difference between moving forward productively and simply unleashing a flood of uncontrolled dumping. We suspect the latter is what raises fear in leaders' hearts and minds, resulting in the decision not to raise issues in the first place. This brings us to a critical distinction. Merely having feelings is not the problem. How we *act* on our feelings (our behaviour) can and should be subject to scrutiny. Those who express anger through temper tantrums should be held accountable for acting out. Neither petulant outbursts nor sulky moodiness have a place in business settings. Our point is that if we encourage people to bring their whole selves to work, we can expect emotions to show up. It is a natural part of being human and cannot be avoided.

Let us share with you—based on our many experiences as facilitators—what happens when feelings are submerged. Contrary to popular belief, they do not conveniently disappear. They go from what is called *overt* (visible and available for being worked through) to *covert* (hidden and difficult to access). We call this slippage of emotions moving from being "on the table" (overt) to "under the table" (covert). Trust us when we say that once emotions have gone under the so-called table, they become painstaking to excavate.

Once the downward cycle of no longer admitting feelings toward each other has begun, the facilitator (leader) needs to be like a dental surgeon, pulling teeth to get people to open up and risk honestly talking about anything feeling-related. By the way, if feelings are located "above the table," this is also an issue—it means people feel that speaking their unspoken hopes and dreams (the "above" part) is too lofty to put "on the table." Therefore, the goal in working with processes is always to facilitate having the covert become overt (on the table), so that it can be openly dealt with.

In one situation this meant creating a forum, where we spent weeks conducting a series of meetings with two teams, so pent-up upsets could be safely expressed and dealt with. In the first meeting, we allowed only the support group to share their concerns and feelings about operations; operations' role was to listen attentively and take notes. At the next meeting, we reversed roles. At the third meeting, each team came up with action-oriented responses to one another's points. Because feelings and factual business issues had become so enmeshed, it was important to address individuals' personal needs as well as business needs if we were to restore more effective working relationships. To ignore either side of the equation would have meant an incomplete solution.

If this series of meetings strikes you as labour-intensive, it was. At the same time, this level of exchange was absolutely necessary, given how broken the interactions were. In our experience, communication breakdowns must be explicitly declared, which is precisely what failed to happen due to both team leaders' discomfort with conflict and emotional upset. Afraid of "discussing the undiscussables," they heightened tension by hoping it would miraculously clear up if ignored. They assumed employees would magically speak up to each other directly if they had something to say. This did not happen. At best, people declared their frustrations behind one another's backs and never to the person with whom they had the actual issue.

Instead, these leaders needed to teach people that feelings are healthy. They needed to take the lead in drawing out emotions and make it easy for employees to express their points of view. What was needed was a specific method for moving from the communication *breakdown* into a communication *breakthrough* (defined as a new possibility for how to interact more effectively). First, people needed to be shown how to be explicit in describing the situation and their feelings. This is called "declaring a communication breakdown." Without making each other 'wrong,' they needed to describe the more positive behaviours they saw missing from their interactions. Next, there needed to be a commitment to define and produce a new reality (the communication breakthrough) by learning to make requests of each other, followed by action on the promises made. This is the nature of the clear agreements we helped these teams and their leaders make.

Another example of when it is critical for leaders to invite the expression of all emotions—anger, fear, discouragement, doubt and anxiety—is during transitions. Transitions are defined by William Bridges in *Managing Transitions* as the psychological process people go through to come to terms with a new situation. Periods of intense change naturally create transitions in employees' lives and therefore must be handled with great care if people's hearts and souls are to stay engaged. For instance, if employees cannot voice the losses that come with transitions, they will neither process painful Endings, nor be completely able to embrace the new possibilities associated with change—which is what they are being asked to do. Endings always precede New Beginnings (opposite to how change is typically executed), often with a period of intense ambiguity and confusion in the middle. Transitions are no time for the proverbial stiff upper lip. If anything, unspoken dictates to hold emotions in check are probably the greatest disservice done to people at work, for tears are vital to clearing emotions.

In fact, the tremendous power of voicing emotions during cultural transformation was unequivocally demonstrated to us when working with our client to train a group of administrative assistants to embrace challenging new responsibilities. Although our client was highly attuned to the company's emotional climate, it was still surprising to witness the amount of venting that needed to be released once we got the group together. Gathered for the first time around one table, this disparate group of individuals pounced on the opportunity to have someone simply listen with respect to how they were feeling. As the training session unfolded, it became very clear our work together was as much, if not more, about expressing their emotions than it was about the actual program itself. In other words, we could have done no training at all, and the day would have been a success simply through letting people give voice to their emotions.

In another example, we were charged with spearheading an intervention where business unit leaders and human resources specialists traveled across North America to support call centre agents whose roles were being consolidated into a new, centralized environment. No one was considering how this mammoth change would impose on employees' lives, only the logistics of closing the offices (e.g., technology, leases, furniture and equipment). Presumably, leaders concluded we were dealing with a young workforce, so the impact should not be large. While true in one sense, this does not mitigate human beings' need to come to terms with Endings (no matter what their age group) and be assisted to move on by talking about their futures.

As it turns out, this process proved so powerful in the cities that we led the same discussions with the company's head office employees. A supportive President and CEO recognized the importance of engaging in transitions dialogues with everyone. So we co-conducted these sessions. We encouraged employees to donate memorabilia to a time capsule and articulate remembrances as the organization marked its ten-year anniversary. This really helped employees who were struggling with ending that period in the company's history to embrace the coming wave of organizational growth. Such sensitivity is characteristic of soul-inspiring leaders. They promote, along with the entire leadership team, a climate of disclosure, frankness and release.

High in EQ, or "emotional intelligence," soul-inspiring leaders listen with empathy when dealing with their own and others' feelings. Such leaders demonstrate understanding of team members' surface words as well as the underlying feelings by listening for emotions along with facts. When we coach leaders, we constantly remind them to respond to both what is and is not being said. The latter is especially important. We have them do this by reflecting back the emotion being expressed by the other person (e.g., upset, tension, etc.) as well as the stated points of conversation (the actual words).

Empathy does not mean sympathy, however. Sympathy is being affected by another's state by adopting their feelings, while empathy denotes compassionately understanding another's condition without actually experiencing their emotions. Here is how this difference played out in two leaders with whom we worked. In the first case, a team leader communicated an overhaul of shift schedules in a "*There, there, dear. I'm so sorry the company is doing this to you*" way (sympathy). In the second instance, the team leader recognized not everyone was happy with the changes, but problem-solved with direct reports to adjust to the new situation (empathy).

Emotionally capable leaders dispel several myths. They throw on its ear the old adage that displaying feelings is a sign of weakness. They demonstrate that leaders do not have to be aloof and analytical to be effective. They empathize both passionately and realistically with people, and care intensely about the work employees do. Soul-inspiring leaders do not leave their emotions at home. They recognize one does not have to be the cold-hearted boss to be respected. It is not necessary to choose between being liked and respected; one can have both.

What is unrealistic is separating emotions and business. People are both thinking and feeling beings. To force them to be only one way on the job is to reinforce unnatural either-or distinctions. Squelching emotions dampens spirits, while being honest about feelings helps souls sing and sets hearts free. As you consider how you can allow for emotions to be a natural yet appropriate part of the workplace, think about this definition of a day well lived: one in which you have laughed, cried, and learned something.

QUESTIONS FOR REFLECTION

- To what extent do you allow yourself to show your true feelings at work? Are there any feelings you consider inappropriate to display in business?
- What do you honestly think of others who freely demonstrate a full range of emotion at work?
- What is the strongest feeling you have about your organization?

DO'S AND DON'TS

- **Do** be fearless in "discussing the undiscussables."
- **Do** make space for the full expression of emotions, particularly during times of transition and cultural transformation.
- **Do** listen for emotions along with facts.
- **Do not** confuse sympathy with empathy.
- **Do not** believe having feelings is the problem; how people act on their feelings can be subject to scrutiny.

- **Do not** allow emotions to go from "overt" (visible and available for processing) to "covert" (hidden and difficult to access).

EXERCISE FOR TEAM LEARNING

Have each member of your team record in their journals daily for a week (including the weekend) five statements describing their emotions for that day. Statements should be feeling-oriented, not a description of what people thought about the situations they recorded. At the end of the week, have everyone look over their thirty-five statements to discern any patterns (e.g., repeated feelings, predominant emotions). Use your next team meeting to discuss how it *felt* to do this exercise. Ask each person if they would continue it, and why or why not.

FIRST STEPS ALONG THE WAY

Assigned Task	Expected Outcome
Train all employees in conflict resolution skills, including the art of declaring communication breakdowns and creating breakthroughs. This step can combine classroom training and on-the-job learning with coaching by facilitators who can lead them through difficult conversations.	*Offers a common language for resolving issues. Encourages employees to use similar methods to resolve issues. If the steps combine discussion of feelings and their impact, plus ways to fully work through issues, results in win-win outcomes on previously unsolvable problems.*
Consider adopting a "talking stick" methodology during meetings. The object can be anything you choose, as long as it can be easily passed around a group (we have used batons and stones in the past). The person who has the talking stick has the floor and cannot be interrupted.	*Gives everyone a turn at sharing thoughts and feelings—particularly if you are concerned some members will hold back their views. Creates order out of what might otherwise feel like chaos by preventing everyone from speaking at once. Gives people a chance to be heard before the team moves into problem solving.*

Fun

> We all procrastinate at one time or another. The most unfortunate procrastination of all is to put off being happy.
>
> —Maureen Mueller

How does one build workplaces where people are not just allowed, but invited, to have fun? It starts with wanting people to feel alive. As a leader, you must first be open to creating uplifting environments, knowing these workplaces attract the bright and enthusiastic employees you seek to hire and retain. The tone and tenor you set is directly connected to your own belief systems about fun at work. Do you believe people accomplish more and better results while infused with spirit, or does productivity in your mind equate with nose-to-the-grindstone seriousness? While seemingly a minor point, your comfort zone greatly impacts whether your employees liberate their own free and easygoing natures—

what one psychology theory refers to as the fun "Inner Child." Each of us has one; it is just a matter of whether we feel comfortable enough letting him or her out.

Anticipating you want to bring more fun into people's work lives, do not assume it means paying big bucks for one-time events. Fun is not necessarily a splashy gala where a powerhouse motivational speaker is flown in to jazz up the troops at the company's annual meeting. On the contrary—a morning of belly-laughs with a humour consultant, only to return to a slave-like environment of disabling workloads and single-digit morale, leaves more damage in its wake than if you had not gone to the expense in the first place.

Happily, joy is easily ignited by building fun into daily routines. In that vein, let us share a playful idea we once instituted called the Comedy Corner. It was a basket of toys like bubble-blowing liquid, puzzles, a magic wand, fortune-telling games and Silly Putty. You would not believe how something so simple could have brought so many people to the Comedy Corner to enjoy a play break! Over time, colleagues donated their own contributions to the toy chest, making for a very eclectic grouping of objects. Warner Bros. animator Chuck Jones echoed the important connection between play and work some years ago while being honoured as a Lifetime Achievement Award recipient during an Academy Awards T.V. broadcast. He considered himself deeply privileged that his work afforded so much opportunity to play, making his avocation (hobby) and vocation (work) one. That's what we are going for here!

Understandably, you may wonder what a collection of children's paraphernalia possibly has to do with efficiency and effectiveness. With such distractions, do you fear no work will get done? Admittedly, we carefully defined the boundaries between our "funky" culture and high-performance expectations in the environment described. One does not negate the other. It is essential that everyone clearly understands these distinctions, so chaos is not let loose. Once addressed though, let the fun begin! As it turns out, we found team members returned to their tasks with renewed vigour after a visit to the Comedy Corner, dispelling the myth that fun and productivity do not co-exist.

In addition, celebration of achievements is constant in soul-inspiring workplaces. Leaders in these organizations do not wait for business initiatives to be completed before encouraging employees to relish their successes. Acknowledging progress at key milestones can be as simple as giving an afternoon off or inviting employees and their partners to enjoy a meal on the company. Such interventions promote a second wind that gives everyone the momentum to push to the finish line. If anything, marking accomplishments only after months of grueling effort results in a kind of "lunch bag letdown," as in "*we had to wait all this time to finally recognize all our hard work?*" More than anticlimactic, waiting until large-scale undertakings end to acknowledge the *select few* rather than the *contributory many* becomes depressingly demotivating. Not only does failure to celebrate along the way set up an inhumane dynamic where people are pressed to the breaking point, it reveals a fear mentality on the part of hard-driving leaders—namely, that people cannot be trusted to persevere if we allow too much fun early in the project life cycle. Talk about the antithesis of joy!

Another great example of celebration comes in the form of Graduation Day from an intensive training program for call centre agents in a start-up operation to which we provided consulting expertise. Given high expectations for their performance, these agents' graduation was a big deal. Everyone in the business unit was invited to the ceremony—to share inspiring words of welcome and to reinforce the culture we were dedicated to building together. As more groups completed training, these celebrations took on a life of their own, with the focus shifting from senior leaders sharing words of wisdom to new hires volunteering their personal observations. Surrounded by balloons, streamers, gifts and cake, each group appointed a valedictorian, followed by readings of favourite quotes from each team member.

Here is an excerpt from a speech delivered by just one graduating class:

> *We entered this environment, students of life… only to become teachers of understanding…. Together we have grown from children to adolescents in knowledge. I feel this company is our child, to nurture it while it grows to its potential worldwide…. In closing, I won't welcome my fellow trainees and teammates (it's been done!); instead, I welcome (the company) to us, and what will prove to be a paradigm shift toward (the company's) global presence.*

These are profound words from a new hire of a mere four weeks. We find it remarkable that such a short-tenured employee would so enthusiastically take on responsibility to pay back the organization's training investment in him so quickly after being hired. We believe his attitude is a real testament to the contributory power that gets unleashed when soul-inspiring leaders purposefully create an environment where people are celebrated for bringing their whole selves to work.

Even team-building events do not singularly need to be skills development-oriented in order to have business impact. For example, it is easy to remember the special camaraderie generated among a group of newly hired leaders simply by encouraging the unit's director to deliberately design get-to-know-each-other time into the weekend retreat we helped him plan. Arriving on a Friday, everyone was treated to spa appointments, followed by a welcome meal. We then facilitated an after-dinner whole group conversation we called Fireside Chats, during which specific questions created the structure to draw out sharing about each person's qualities, talents, working styles and preferences—information that laid the highly useful groundwork for us to create a vision and set of values with this leadership team during the 'formal' part of the retreat.

While it may all seem very elite, we can reassure you from our experiences as organizational development consultants, more team building was accomplished during that one conversation than was gained through all the beautifully orchestrated agenda content over the next two days. By thoughtfully creating a particular atmosphere with our client-director, we brought out in this team lasting connections that sped everyone's integration and set in place the people foundation so critical to business success.

Finally, why not consider bringing people together for no particular reason at all? If you need an excuse, occasions like Halloween, company picnics, team sports and charitable community events offer many a sense of childlike enjoyment. Opportunities to introduce spirit are limited only by your imagination.

We still remember the day we concocted the notion of transforming an unused overhead projector stand into a Bar and Beverage cart that we wheeled from office to office, serving our colleagues fun mixes of fresh fruit juices. People just howled with delight at the zaniness of our idea, and it released a floodgate of thoughtfulness from other leaders that extended throughout the day—including an office pizza lunch, afternoon ice cream bars and licorice-string treats—all because we tapped into what was clearly a pent-up desire to let loose and have fun. You cannot imagine our joy at seeing these other leaders hop onto the bandwagon (or, in this case, the Bar and Beverage cart)! The point is, laughter rings daily throughout soul-inspiring workplaces. People are able to lighten up enough to enjoy spontaneous humorous moments and shared jokes, or to look upon their foibles with unabashed delight.

And what of laughter's benefits? Could it be that humour and fun increase productivity? We ascribe to this notion. In fitness circles, the positive effects of endorphins released through exercise are well documented. So, why would this not hold true emotionally, mentally and spiritually through laughter at work? In causing spirits to soar and minds to wander, laughter promotes creativity. Like children at play, adults release innovation through fun. Given the imperatives to increase out-of-the-box thinking and decrease escalating stress-management costs, we suggest you have your business case for putting fun first.

Consider that the average four-year-old laughs fifty times a day, while the average adult laughs only fifteen times. Perhaps if we found more ways to apply fun and laughter to our work, it would be less like an albatross and more like a source of spontaneity and joy. Given how many hours we spend at work, doesn't it make sense to have that time be as pleasant as possible?

QUESTIONS FOR REFLECTION

- Do you consider your workplace fun? What elements contribute to, or take away, fun for you?
- Do you believe it is OK to have fun at work? How do your belief systems influence your colleagues' sense of fun?
- What kinds of tasks and environments cause your energy to be drained away, and what types enhance your energy?

DO'S AND DON'TS

- **Do** build fun into daily routines by stretching your imagination for creative ideas.
- **Do** build fun time into team-building events and know this will help you reach your business objectives.
- **Do** bring people together for fun for no reason at all.
- **Do not** wait for massive projects to end before you take time to celebrate.
- **Do not** acknowledge only the *select few* when you celebrate; remember the *contributory many.*

EXERCISE FOR TEAM LEARNING

Invite several volunteers from your team during your next budget-setting exercise to provide input to a line item called Morale, or Fun, which would be used to spend money on what employees define as fun. Bring this thinking forward to the senior management team, so that at their next meeting, every leader is charged with using his or her full monetary allotment over the prescribed period. Part of the agreement will be that senior leaders make this an ongoing agenda item during their regular meetings, to ensure that the monies are being used across the organization.

FIRST STEPS ALONG THE WAY

Assigned Task	*Expected Outcome*
Taking your reflections about what is fun and energy-enhancing for you, brainstorm ten sets each of: less than five-minute fun breaks (short), fifteen-minute breaks (medium), half-hour to hour-long breaks (longer). Over a series of ten weeks, plot out a schedule by which you will incorporate at least one short, one medium and one longer break into your calendar each week.	*Stretches your creativity muscles in coming up with clever ways to build fun into your daily routine. This exercise challenges you to overcome the objection of not having enough time, because you can fill out your schedule over a series of weeks.*

Institute company-wide quarterly Play Days, like the track & field days you used to have in public school. Design several options into these getaway days, so everyone can find at least one activity in which to participate that they consider fun (our personal definitions vary).

Results in everyone taking semi-regular time for fun and rejuvenation, and builds some team spirit in the process. Some people get so stuck on the treadmill of serious businesslike professionalism, it is as if they need to be given permission to let their hair down once in a while.

Grace

> **Blessed are those who can give without remembering, and take without forgetting.**
>
> **—Princess Elizabeth Asquith Bibesco**

All great leaders demonstrate grace—the ability to rise above pettiness, to forgive and forget, to restrain and reserve opinions. This essential attitude helps eliminate the fear of failure present in so many followers. Without tolerance for failure, we become risk-averse and unimaginative.

This is best illustrated by a client story of a market-leading firm that believed strongly in its culture of open-mindedness that inspired employees to achieve all of which they were capable. The cornerstone of this belief was a mission and set of values statements that included, among others, a desire for employees to take risks and be entrepreneurial.

Since the company had a stated intention to attract and retain high performers, promoting such a culture made sense—especially for creative types who stretch the limits of what is possible. And while they more often than not succeed, they also fail. Early in the company's history, this was an accepted part of running the business; experimentation was expected and tolerated. Some things didn't work, but learning took place and generally results improved. This tolerance for failure and acceptance of effort (not simply results) is a critical element of grace in organizational settings and it was a crucial underpinning of this company's culture.

However, as markets grew more competitive and revenues stopped growing at their previous rate, there was a typical knee-jerk reaction from leadership: they announced a program to "*focus on results*." We were not present at meetings where this issue was discussed, so we are unable to ascertain if there was deliberate dialogue about the potential impact of this upon the company's culture—something easily defined as an asset that had been a major driver of performance. However, we are sure nobody cared enough about it to resist the urge to make the announcement.

The outcome over the next year or so is a predictable tale: the phrase "*focus on results*" became code-speak for a move toward short-term thinking, efforts to boost sales at the expense of customers and intense pressure on key staff. The environment quickly became a pressure-cooker and inevitably, the innovation that had been so much a part of the organization's past began to ebb away. It had the opposite effect from the results management intended. People became reluctant to take charge; fear of failure made them risk-averse. They began to look over their shoulders and wonder what was being whispered in the shadows about them. They started looking for the "sure bets" that would deliver what the company now seemed to value—predictable but mediocre results.

This loss of grace resulted in a cultural shift that put the company on a collision course with failure. For, just as they tightened up, the competition continued to push the envelope and gain momentum. By the second year of this story, the company faced near panic-stricken management who, trapped by results, now moved into what we refer to as the blame game. They began to determine what they referred to as the "*weak links*" in the organization, that were not focusing on results, and fired them. A more recently-hired group of leaders was replaced by an old guard, who immediately re-implemented the very same human resources practices that had caused employees several years earlier to retaliate against this business by voting in a union. Destroying the remnants of newer leaders' creations resulted in significant rework on policies, programs and practices already proven highly effective among the workforce. What an expensive rehashing exercise.

Yet all this was seen by leadership as an effort to send a message to the troops about the need for accountability and to ensure everyone recognized "*how serious the situation is.*" Does any of this sound familiar? By no means is this the only company where we have seen this occur.

What did not happen in this example is a graceful acceptance that results and effort are not always the same thing. It is truly possible for a company to be running at 110 percent capacity, fully staffed by dedicated people, and for the business not to achieve its planned results. This was precisely the case in another organization. Initially a founder-run firm, it grew by leaps and bounds over an intense two-year period by doubling its staff size in a number of key functions and eventually merging with another company. And yet, despite the increased capacity attained by augmenting the talent pool, and despite everyone's truly superhuman efforts on a daily basis, results actually declined to worrisome lows over this same period.

How can it be that people are working this hard and yet their efforts fail to translate to the bottom line? For the very reason, we suggest, that when businesses set out to define "expected results," they are really no more than an invention of that organization's best sense about the marketplace. As targets or objectives set at the beginning of some period, they are built on certain assumptions about markets, prices, customers and competitors. And, while many times these assumptions will be right, they can also be wrong.

Unanticipated events can make plans difficult or impossible to achieve—as was the case in both of our examples. Apart from broader internal systemic issues that plagued both firms, what they could not have fairly factored into their calculations were significant industry trends that hugely dampened their ability to prosper. Instead, both companies needed to reset their 'compass,' so leadership could help people find "true north" again and regain market control through continued innovation. Ironically, the first company—as a wholly private firm—actually had this opportunity, but chose not to exercise it, much to its own ultimate detriment. In the second instance, senior leadership needed to step up to the plate by providing a clear vision and strong direction, as well as sales targets more in keeping with the realities of an incomplete merger.

Let us make a point here. We recognize the cost of failing to "make plan" is steep, especially in companies whose stocks are traded on public markets. Punished by analysts, market-makers and the media, any company that does not make plan is instantly on its way to disaster. Who has not read of these accounts in the business media in the recent past?

Rather than forgiving and forgetting and encouraging companies to press forward, these collective actions encourage them to retrench and focus on what they know. The consequence of this lack of grace is to drive the organization toward a death spiral. In this situation, some of us can find parallels in our experiences as children, yet we have failed to translate these basic lessons into our workplaces.

Reflect back, perhaps to a period where you were learning a new skill, sport or having trouble with a subject in school. Surely your parents, coaches and teachers did not give up and focus on what you already knew. Surely the more appropriate response was to reward effort, not just results, and to keep focusing on the path that eventually got you to where you wanted to be. Imagine how different our development would be if we learned early in life that the price of failure was to either stop trying or be stopped from trying again. Or, reflect on how difficult life is for any of your friends who are so risk-averse that they live in a dry, contained world; there, they strive to control everything, in order to feel artificially successful. The sheer depth of their underachievement—in contrast to what they may have been capable of—is often striking to the rest of us, but goes unacknowledged by the victims of this torturous existence. This is yet another instance of what can happen when we are not surrounded by grace.

Therefore, one needs to think carefully about environments too structured or filled with artificial expectations to enable a healthy balance between focus on results and experimentation; where grace is demonstrated toward effort as well as results. We do not have a magical solution for this conundrum. It requires wholesale change in the behaviour and attitudes of institutions on a scale we are not sure can be achieved until there is also large-scale institutional awareness of the problem. We are not naïve enough to believe the simplicity of our ideas will suddenly sweep world markets and make them more forgiving. Nor are we trying to assert that mediocrity should be rewarded with undue patience, as some may choose to interpret our comments. We are simply standing by a principle of a balanced view of performance we believe should be more characterized by gracious rather than institutional traits. For those of you who have a chance to make a difference in this realm, we invite you to forgive easily and quickly, demonstrating grace toward those who tried and failed as well as those who succeeded. Grace under pressure wins the day!

QUESTIONS FOR REFLECTION

- What connections do you see between a feeling of safety from being judged solely on your results and your ability to be creative?
- What kind of impact do you think more grace could have on your workplace and on your relationships?
- How does the environment in which you were raised influence your reaction to this chapter and your ability to demonstrate grace toward others?

DO'S AND DON'TS

- Do remember that results and effort are not always the same thing.
- Do demonstrate tolerance for failure and acceptance of effort (not simply results).
- Do balance focus on results and experimentation.
- **Do not** engage in the "blame game" when people's efforts fail; learn from what happened without punishing people.
- **Do not** retrench and focus on what you know in the face of failure.

EXERCISE FOR TEAM LEARNING

At your next team meeting, have each direct report identify the person they know who most demonstrates the quality of grace in either their personal or professional life. Have them think about specific examples of acts that made them choose this person. What does this person do, and why, that makes this trait so obvious to them? Go around the group one by one and have people report their findings, speaking also to whether their selected role model's behaviours could be a guiding light for their own transformation toward more grace.

FIRST STEPS ALONG THE WAY

Assigned Task	*Expected Outcome*
Reflect on how you could demonstrate more grace in your life in ways that would be recognizable to those around you.	*Begins the process of noticing when your own responses are filled with grace versus when they are not. Since grace starts within us, this is a good place to start.*
If you feel trapped by organizational forces beyond your control, with regard to demonstrating grace and higher tolerance for failure, identify these barriers and reflect on them carefully. Try and deal with them as best you can, while still seeking ways within your domain of control to increase grace.	*Avoids the trap of relying on uncontrollable external factors as an excuse for not attempting to increase grace in areas where you can. In such a challenging area, it is important to gain whatever control you can.*

Heart

> **We can choose to make our love for each other what our lives are really about.**
> —Werner Erhard

Reflect for a moment how often business language refers to the heart—"*getting to the heart of the matter*," "*what lies at the heart of the issue*," "*to have a change of heart*"—to name but a few. Notice the origin of the word "courage:" *cor*, standing for heart. To have courage means to have heart. When we encourage others, offering them courage, we literally give them heart.

One of the most eloquent stories we know about bringing heartfelt compassion to work comes from the cardiac floor of a hospital. As a dangerous-looking biker was wheeled into Emergency receiving, everyone looked toward Bonnie, the head nurse, silently pleading to not be given this untouchable to bathe. A consummate leader, Bonnie stepped forward to tend the unkempt man herself. Offering a highly unconventional backrub, she reached out to this man rejected by life's rudeness. As her gentle ministering ended, the biker had tears running down his cheeks. In a quivering voice, he said, "*No one has touched me for years. Thank you.*"[1]

As both our opening quote and story suggest, we can either interact with the world from fear or love—including the arena of work. So why is it we seem to raise such intense discomfort when coaching leaders about the benefits of bringing their own hearts to work and encouraging others to do the same? More often met with panic than willingness, we find leaders want nothing more than to shirk this responsibility.

Repeatedly, we receive fear-based objections like, "*How can I be caring without being taken advantage of?*" The mere thought of demonstrating more heart at work engenders a brusque confrontation on the order of: "*My job calls for me to be tough. How can you possibly ask me to be loving when I must make decisions that cause people pain or when I have to be the final authority on a decision?*" as if the act of showing kindness to employees would somehow render leaders foolish or impotent—swallowing them in the dog-eat-dog business world.

The net result of this fear-based dynamic in most organizations is that the head rules the roost. "*I think, therefore I am*" has become the credo of left brain-dominated workplaces, underpinned by the belief logic alone will result in productivity. The heart is viewed as somehow soft and therefore unnecessary (if not a detriment) to success. One consequence of this head-over-heart dynamic is that much of organizational life is out of balance. Admittedly, keeping both the head and heart alive in business represents a leadership paradox.

At both individual and collective levels, our goal should be to create a state of harmony that can only be achieved by training our heads to acknowledge the wisdom and compassion of our hearts. We are not advocating one over the other; we need both. In our consultations with one organization, we helped coin the phrase "common sense business leader with heart" as a way to reconcile these apparently contradictory notions. We used it to denote the integration of mind, body and spirit at work. Rather than an either-or solution, it is an all-encompassing mode where the head and heart together serve the hands to execute leadership tasks.

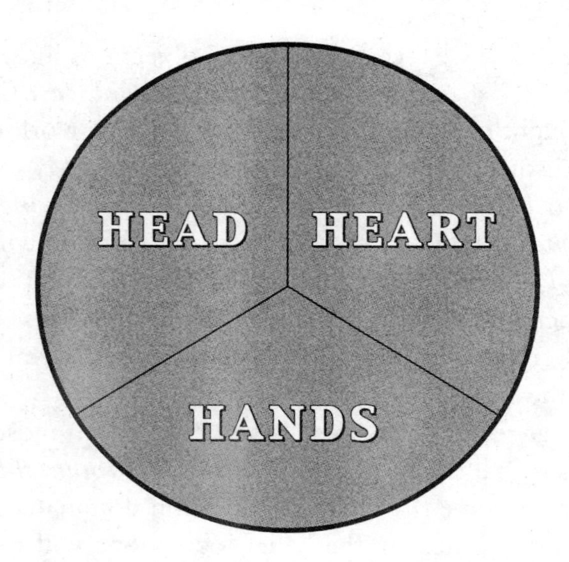

- *The head (common sense)* represents the scientific, rational, logical, linear mode of thought. The head is focused on planning, organizing, analyzing, problem-solving and decision-making—core management skills forming the foundation of Western business thinking. To operate strictly with heart while ignoring the head is as imbalanced as its opposite.

- The leader ***with heart*** is not afraid to get close to people, demonstrating his or her genuine caring and interest in others. These leaders know the more one accepts both self and others, the more there is a sense of heart across the whole organization—evidenced in compassion and understanding.

- Leaders who use their ***hands*** are doers, in the best sense. Not hesitant to get his or her hands dirty, like Bonnie, this leader rolls up his or her own sleeves during times of high pressure, stress and crisis. Wanting to understand life in the trenches, this leader conducts regular temperature-checks by walking around and talking with people on the front lines.

Inviting the many benefits of the heart into business is a powerful force in achieving high standards and stretch goals. The best leaders with whom we have worked and coached achieve their stellar results precisely because they pay attention to the heart. If anything, we find time and again in our consulting practices that outwardly gruff leaders ultimately become what we call beloved—those for whom people will give their all. Beneath their blustery exteriors lie hearts of gold. Even when their actions would not be deemed loving (for example, laying off their workforce), these leaders realize they can still approach obligatory tasks in either fear- or love-based ways. In this context, heart brings forth images of courage when faced with great challenges and hope when confronted with great difficulties. It involves strength and toughness. It involves leaders' awareness of their responsibilities to those they are entrusted to lead, and to the values of the organizations that selected them. It is the dichotomy between toughness and tenderness, guts and grace, fairness and firmness.

If the word 'love' still causes you discomfort in a workplace context, remember it can be embodied through feelings of affection and deeds of friendliness, helping out, sharing, understanding, tolerance, cooperation and teamwork. While some may not immediately think of these as loving acts, we find it hard to imagine that any but the most callous leaders would take issue with these words. Something else we know for certain: encouraging others to open their hearts at work cannot be delegated. Leaders must start by modeling kindness themselves.

Heart-centred thinkers know that love is powerful. It transforms everyone in its presence and overcomes even the steepest challenges. Not surprisingly, science is now underscoring these notions with measurable data. For example, one Institute of HeartMath study shows our hearts are the strongest amplifying system we have for generating positive electrical fields; when laboratory subjects augmented attention to their hearts with feelings of appreciation and caring, computer printouts displayed expanding circles of energy emanating from their hearts.[2]

Of course, being a believer does not automatically a doer make. Activating the power of our hearts takes practice and consistent intention. We strengthen our heart muscle through willingness. While invisible to the eye, make no mistake: the health of a company's 'heart' is felt at the core of everyone's being—through outward-rippling effects on employees, shareholders, customers and suppliers.

For those who might wonder what love and heart have to do with profits and earnings—the supposed reasons organizations are in business—we simply state that leaders who capture their employees' hearts seldom need to worry about the motivation to produce exactly these outcomes. Engaged hearts motivate themselves. Forward-looking organizations do everything in their power to assist leaders and employees to integrate body (hands), mind (head) and spirit (heart) in ways that produce exceptional results far surpassing any financial forecast dreamt up by the brain alone.

QUESTIONS FOR REFLECTION

- What is one thing you have done in the last week to send a signal to people that welcoming the heart at work is important to you?
- What proportions of your life do you spend coming from your head, heart and hands—and what do you notice about these percentages?
- How much would you say you 'love' the people you lead, the products and services you offer, and the customers or clients you serve?

DO'S AND DON'TS

- **Do** be a "common sense business leader with heart."
- **Do** balance mind, body and spirit in the workplace, and encourage others to do the same.
- **Do** remember you can approach even obligatory

tasks in either fear- or love-based ways; you have the power to choose.

- **Do not** overlook that modeling heartfelt kindness starts with you.
- **Do not** fall into the trap of feeling you have to be tough to be respected.

EXERCISE FOR TEAM LEARNING

Together with your team members and/or leadership colleagues, develop your own definition of the "common sense business leader with heart." Break the phrase into the following elements: *common sense* (head), *business leader* (hands), *with heart* (heart). Use the definitions we provided, even while focusing on how these characteristics would be demonstrated behaviourally in your workplace. Make it specific to your environment. Develop a set of agreements, so that people will see and feel your commitment through words and actions. Let them know you expect to be 'called' on your behaviour (i.e., having it pointed out to you), if you are not being this kind of leader. Also, challenge your team to demonstrate these same behaviours through their personal leadership, even if they do not hold a management title.

FIRST STEPS ALONG THE WAY

Assigned Task	Expected Outcome
Consider that we can interact with the world by either being cold- or warm-hearted. Be rigorous with yourself in determining the degree to which you are each of these in your life overall.	*Engaging in reflection of this sort ultimately lays the groundwork for changing your own 'heart' energy in lasting ways. Being willing to do a personal exercise of this sort demonstrates your commitment to being more open to the wisdom of the heart (and not just the brain).*
Recall the classic children's tale by Dr. Seuss, *How the Grinch Stole Christmas.* Brainstorm for yourself the series of events that led up to the Grinch's heart growing from a shriveled ball into a radiant sunburst.	*Strengthens your own heart's expansion and develops ideas on how you can continuously strengthen your heart muscle in the world. Using what you learn can expand the ways 'heart' shows up in your workplace.*

NOTES

[1] Canfield, Jack et al. *Chicken Soup for the Soul at Work.* Deerfield Beach: Health Communications Inc., 1996.

[2] Thoele, Sue Patton. *The Woman's Book of Soul.* Berkeley: Conari Press, 1998.

Imagination

> No pessimist ever discovered the secrets of the stars, or sailed to an uncharted land, or opened a new heaven to the human spirit.
>
> —Helen Keller

Imagination should be a requirement for becoming a leader. Or rather, for becoming a *good* leader, since organizations are full of leaders deemed successful by their employers, but clearly lacking in imagination. Why is this so? We begin life so full of imagination, able to think freely and creatively, and associate ourselves with almost limitless possibilities. Slowly, we become proud of our ability to think rationally—to put boundaries around our thinking. This skill takes over and we lose our appreciation for the magic of imagination.

But imagination is a powerful force that can open up possibilities and allow us to see beyond current circumstances into a future state not yet realized. Is that not the essence of leadership—to outline a promised future compelling for all people to participate in?

The best illustration we have for the huge impact of a leader's loss of imagination can be found at a seminar we were leading a few years ago. The topic was improving productivity in the workplace and this particular public session was graced with the presence of the President of a well-known North American company. He listened politely to our content and even asked the odd question along the way—all very appropriate, until we hit a section on managing performance through goal setting.

What hit him so hard was a quote used to set up this section, which provokes leaders to really think about goals. Viktor Frankl was quoted as saying a goal was *"a dream with a deadline."* The underlying implication, that leaders must dream dreams and be prepared to use their imaginations to envision the future, provoked an immediate rise from the President. He insisted this was the most dangerous thing he had ever heard. In his view, responsible leaders had to learn to set boundaries for their often wayward organizations to ensure they could execute the vision. If that was to occur, surely it had to be realistic (meaning "within reach"). Time spent on "dreaming" was time spent "day-dreaming" in his estimation.

We did not argue with his perspective, since it was probably shared by many in the room. Not that we agreed; it is just that they had a view of themselves as "managing performance" and so did we! There are legions of consultants teaching folks how to do that, and the tactics often focus on exactitude. Nobody looked for us to introduce the fuzzy aspects of imagination and creative leadership, which are "*too hard to measure*." Surely they felt we needed a deliberate strategy and easy-to-understand tactics that would translate into the troops all moving in the same direction—didn't we?

This very view, in our minds, distinguishes the debate about management versus leadership. In organizations the world over, you do not have to be a leader in order to be a manager. Under the circumstances noted above, anybody can manage, since the task is about tactical execution—getting people to do things right. Of course, we could debate as to whether they are doing the *right* things. We all know how easy it is to feel as though we are working exceptionally hard to do things right, and yet there still seems to be something missing from our days. Could it be that the missing element is a sense of imagination borne of an agreed sentiment that we are also doing the right things—things tied to a higher vision or cause?

In our opinion, it is not possible to claim to be a leader if all you do is manage. Leaders lead, and they lead with vision. And not with any vision, but with a compelling vision of the future—best drawn from the spark of their imaginations. Logic and reason tend to impose boundaries on human potential, as is the case with one leader whom we coached. We acknowledge Marvin for reinforcing with his team the logic of getting things done 'right'—and communicating the immediate rationale for doing so. What was missing in his over-emphasis on rightness was a sense for his personal vision for doing the right things that would have engaged a powerful 'why' in people's minds.

Essentially, he disconnected the "content" from its "context." People seemed to know *what* was expected but not *why*. As soon as we pointed out to Marvin how sharing his vision would actually ignite the very performance he was trying to generate, he shifted his style. He could see that leading from a longer-term strategic perspective would balance what had been a short-term tactical emphasis. As a result, Marvin's team became more engaged than ever, for they now had a compelling vision that both drove their daily actions and incited achievement that far surpassed previous benchmarks. This ability to connect content and context in powerful ways to achieve the vision is an approach soul-inspiring leaders understand completely. They draw broadly from their knowledge of human nature to craft visions that spark followers' imaginations, resulting in superhuman performance that none would have thought possible had they dared to whisper their dreams out loud.

Martin Luther King had a dream. Gandhi bore the hopes and aspirations of a nation. John F. Kennedy ignited the imagination of Americans everywhere. They are truly exemplary leaders who somehow managed to keep a connection between their goals and imaginations. They turned dreams into reality and people willingly followed them, helping create a reality they alone dared cast as possible. The corporate leader at our seminar would have seen no way to identify the tactics making the strategy of a Man on the Moon a reality. So, it should have never found its way into a goal-setting process, let alone into implementation.

This narrow-minded thinking perfectly demonstrates the failure to lead we find in so much of business today. Instead, if we expect to capture people's imaginations and have them embrace the company's vision, it needs to serve some greater good. It might be a vision to change the world by introducing a revolutionary product. In the high-tech world, it is often about advancing the cause of labour or time-saving technology to benefit people. Although the company naturally desires to create wealth in the process, it does so by serving this higher vision. A vision to simply earn money is not lofty. By itself, it is too empty to be inspiring to most people other than perhaps company owners. It is certainly not compelling, although being profitable can be satisfying for everyone involved as proof of good work. Another flaw in making profit a vision is that it positions the proverbial cart before the horse. Instead, we see profit as an outcome, not a goal. Placed inside this context, profit becomes a natural result of doing a number of things right—a by-product of keeping everyone's eye on the North Star, if you will.

Soul-inspiring leaders know this. They are not constrained by a view of the world as it is today, but rather are liberated by a world they want to create. They create surges of excitement by inviting those around them to imagine the possibilities, not the probabilities. Imagination feeds the very soul of these organizations. And they firmly believe their ability to exist is based on a steady diet of new ideas sparked from the imagination of everyone. New ideas are continually sourced by imaginative leaders—from customers, employees, even competitors. They never met an idea they did not like and did not think deserved some time or attention to determine its impact. They also follow a golden rule: the best ideas can come from anywhere.

If you join an organization like this, be prepared to check your title at the door, for everyone is expected to be part of the idea-generation process. Your ideas will be considered as valuable and powerful as anyone's, even the CEO's. While completely open to the expression of ideas, we are not saying soul-inspiring leaders necessarily implement every idea offered up. Rather, they settle on a few that can generate the outcomes to which everyone is committed. In this way, a set of relatively democratically determined winning ideas becomes the focus of the organization's efforts. And when it comes time for execution, all the elements of success are already in place. The barriers and frustrations that exist in so many organizations when new processes are put in place have been avoided, because people have an authentic sense of broad participation in the idea-generation process. And it started with the leader's openness to spark ideas that sparked others, and so on. That is how imagination builds.

Unfortunately, many businesses are set up to meet analysts' expectations and to ensure predictability of results. That is what the game of business is so often about. We also feel it is the single largest impediment to this lesson ever being absorbed by most corporations. Rather than challenging ourselves with real goals, we set targets. Targets are not drawn from our dreams, but from our current experiences. They are about extrapolations and extensions of what we already know, and they are safe predictions of the future—call it a "managed future."

But these kinds of actions do not shape the future. Leaders shape the future by calling us to attempt actions that could fail. But they could also succeed. And this is the magic of real leadership. Drawing from a shared learning experience with a gifted facilitator, we could take this notion even farther by suggesting that the future is in fact "generated." By generated, he meant that the future already exists apart from present reality, for it is not created from what we know, but from another dimension where we do not colour it with either past or present experiences. We can bring that unpolluted future to us in the moment through our imaginations and use it in the now, rather than creating our future based on the limits of what we already know. Now, that is truly using our extensive untapped capabilities to directly influence the course of our lives! Imagine what would be possible if we all worked with and shaped the future in these powerful ways. That is why effective leaders of today need their imaginations now more than ever.

QUESTIONS FOR REFLECTION

- What is compelling for others about the vision you have set forth?
- Have you ever truly dreamed about the possibilities of what you do, including the potential to change the world?
- How can you learn to better engage people's imaginations, and what would happen to your leadership style if you adopted this as a method?

DO'S AND DON'TS

- Do "paint a picture" of the future that is compelling for all.
- Do use your imagination to craft a vision that serves some greater good, and base your leadership on that vision.
- Do radically alter your views so that profit is seen as a by-product rather than the sole purpose of the organization's existence.

- **Do not** believe the best ideas come from only certain parts of the organization; be open to everyone's ideas.
- **Do not** abuse your title as if it entitles your ideas to be accepted over others'.
- **Do not** be constrained by a view of the world as it is today; instead be liberated by the world you want to create.

EXERCISE FOR TEAM LEARNING

In keeping with the concept of creating a "generated" future, lead your team through a "What Is Our Dream" exercise. Create a peaceful and uninterrupted atmosphere where people are encouraged to use right brain techniques (e.g., drawing, using various crafts supplies) to express their hopes and wishes for your business unit or department. Have them apply the art materials to design the To Be (future) picture of what is possible in your group. Have each person share his or her To Be picture, one at a time. After everyone has spoken, encourage people to notice the common themes that have emerged. Record these ideas on flipchart paper and brainstorm with your team the actions that will move you toward The Dream. You can keep returning to and refining this information through subsequent team-building exercises (perhaps as an agenda item part of regularly scheduled team meetings).

FIRST STEPS ALONG THE WAY

Assigned Task	Expected Outcome
Spend time playing games with a child under the age of five.	*Restores your appreciation for imagination.*
Examine your strategic planning and goal-setting processes as an organization. Do they rely on imagination and possibility? Or are they founded upon constrained models of linear thought that fail to call forth an imagined future?	*Encourages "blue sky" (imaginative, right brain) thinking about what is possible in your environment. The ability to influence the goal-setting process within your organization helps restore imagination as the basis for future success.*
Imagine you could forget everything you already knew about what you did and the industry or profession you were a part of. Think of completely new ways of approaching what you do. Imagine also that there is a group of entrepreneurs who are doing exactly this right now and they are six months ahead of you.	*Invites you to set aside left-brain notions by asking you to forget everything you know. Helps you realize the future cannot be created from the past or present; it must be generated from your imagination. Picturing a group of entrepreneurs who are ahead of you creates a sense of urgency in stepping outside of existing constraints.*

Jobs

> **Most of us have jobs that are too small for our spirits.**
>
> **—Studs Terkel**

One area of particular interest to us is the continuing growth in contract and self-employed workers. While the origins of this phenomenon are well documented, it is generally noted that the early '90s trend toward down-sizing and right-sizing broke, once and for all, the traditional employment contract of "jobs for life." It changed forever the post-World War II notion of a benevolent corporation bestowing all one needed, up to and including retirement, in return for loyalty and a diligent work ethic.

One could argue this trend goes back as far as the contract between master and slave, or to the social constructs of serfs and nobility. However, the concept's modern origins probably date to the brilliance of Henry Ford. Those he hired to work on the Model T assembly line in the 1920s—a new concept in manufacturing at the time—often started and ended their careers with Ford. The company created all manner of programs to look after their workers and their families' needs (e.g., building homes, creating clubs, scholarships for children, etc.). Originally, this was done as a means of retaining trained workers in jobs that, truth be known, were not necessarily fulfilling. The jobs did not require creativity or high levels of engagement; only labour and only as strictly prescribed by one's assigned task.

The modern assembly line also gave rise to modern bureaucracy, and eventually to the school of thought known as the Management Sciences. The belief was that most work could be structured and managed as a series of smaller tasks and that management was ultimately responsible for workers' productivity by virtue of how they assigned resources to tasks. Even in the descriptions, we can begin to see how these arrangements run the risk of dehumanizing work and separating workers from their work—the alienation Karl Marx so aptly described. We are not suggesting socialism is the answer to this problem, but we are pointing to issues with the structure of jobs as regards producing results, something we think has been inadequately understood by most organizations.

Jobs need to contain a sense of meaning, challenge and accomplishment. Solid job design means people have the authority to make decisions and perform in flexible ways. We fundamentally believe the person doing the job knows it best—so get out of the way! And, without information about how their contributions impact overall results, team members' motto is likely to be: "*I just do my job and collect my pay.*" Once they can begin saying, "*I see how my actions affect business goals, so I share a responsibility for our collective success*," you have employees who understand what they do, why they do it, and how they make a difference—true performance motivators—as captured in our third Simple Leadership Equation:

SIMPLE LEADERSHIP EQUATION #3:

What + Why + How = Motivated Performance

Nowhere did we come to more fundamentally understand these principles than when we worked with a company that needed (but did not act upon) an almost total overhaul of its job structure. Given the firm's rapid growth, new positions were quickly created to meet emergent demands, but with no attention to what elements would allow candidates being hired into these roles to experience success. Instead, the purportedly new jobs were basically cobbled together by combining into one role a myriad of job functions no one else wanted to perform. This created an overwhelming array of responsibilities virtually impossible for one person alone to fulfill, let alone enjoy any sense of accomplishment. If anything, the unspoken rules for incumbents were to perform their roles exactly as one of the firm's founders would have done—and it was precisely these dictates that flew in the face of everything we know about how to make jobs empowering and motivating. On the other hand, those in longer-standing job functions had been beaten down so often when taking initiative in the past that they had indeed become mere pay-collectors rather than revenue-generators. Nothing the newly-hired staff were expected to do to bump up these support players' motivation levels could have possibly made a lasting difference without leadership recognition of the fatal flaws designed into people's jobs. In each instance, we are talking about the polar opposite of freedom to perform in flexible ways.

Let us go back to the increasing prevalence of people no longer seeking and accepting full-time positions but opting instead for the more challenging path of building their own jobs through contracting and self-employment. We know a full-time job is generally more secure and may be more economically rewarding over the long-term. For many, self-employment and contracting offer only marginal benefits compared to full-time employment. While this is not true for all, and there are exceptions among high-end professions and so-called knowledge workers (e.g., Information Technology), contracting and temporary work have generally been noted as economically less advantageous. Yet, as we have returned to a period of nearly historic employment levels, people have not returned to working full time. They are no longer embracing the traditional job. In fact, they may be rejecting it. Why?

This fact is a stunning condemnation of how we approach job structure. So often, jobs reflect the thinking that people seek only economic gain—they work for pay! We do not believe this traditional thinking will ever solve the "crisis of the soul" that has gripped much of the modern work world. First and foremost, we must acknowledge people's deeply rooted desire for a reasonable amount of satisfying work they are fit to perform. We believe this is the reason so many choose temporary or self-employed work—within these defined boundaries, they find the freedom to be passionate about what they do, and they feel they can achieve a measure of balance they are afraid of losing from their lives if they commit to a full-time position. This does not bode well for businesses as the labour pool continues to shrink.

This problem is not new, but it does require new thinking if we are to come to a place that will allow both the organization and workers to thrive, rather than just survive. So what must happen? We must completely remove our traditional thinking about jobs, since it acts as a constraint on the future possibilities of what restructured work could really look like. Imagine a world where the contract with employees truly rewards results; where employees are proportionately paid for their contribution rather than by title or position. How about a world where status differences between part-time and full-time are irrelevant, as people freely move between periods of less intense and more intense work, based on the natural rhythm of results they need to achieve?

To be successful, we need to get these programs and policies related to job structure out of human resources manuals and embedded into daily life. The sooner senior management takes ownership of these initiatives so they become part of your cultural norm, the sooner you will benefit from employees recognizing you are no longer simply offering jobs, but possibility. Use as your example an organization where one employee made the bold move to approach her leader with the idea of shifting to a four-day work week and was met with an openness of response suggesting she might want to consider a three-day week so as to have even more time to develop her own areas of interest.

Since paving the way with this one simple question, other employees were helped to follow in her footsteps. We wholeheartedly commend the firm's leaders for their willingness to entertain new work options that serve the person, the company and their business goals. This kind of soul-inspiring leadership enables everyone to maximize their own possibilities—and reap the rewards this approach brings with it. The outcome is to open up new levels of productivity, creativity and opportunity for the firm and its workers—the true definition of the new economy 'job' contract.

Finally, organizations must realize that with a shrinking labour pool, there will be fewer individuals willing to take on jobs which are not engaging and fulfilling. Economists speak of the "rise of the knowledge worker." We prefer to talk about the "death of the joe job." With the opportunity that will be generated in the new economy, there will be no need for people to simply hold down a job. Economics will not keep them in positions they find unrewarding. There are simply too many attractive options. In addition, the required economic value-add to justify the average worker's salary in the industrial world will continually raise the bar as far as the jobs we can afford to support. This trend will continue as lower value-adding jobs move to lower-cost parts of the world and the ongoing globalization of world trade thrusts rationalization upon all parts of the economy.

The socio-economic implications for organizations, workers and governments are substantial. Over time, significant social upheaval will occur. It will not be possible to ignore it; it must be understood and dealt with proactively. Failure to do so will only invite chaos as structural economic change overwhelms our ability to keep up and an entire class of angry workers—forced to the sidelines and unable to adapt to the new world of work—becomes the stumbling block to national competitiveness.

Employers and societies cannot ignore changes in the structure of work, and therefore changes taking place in the structure of jobs within the world of work. We must rally our creativity and resources to address these challenges sooner rather than later. We must also work to secure a greater understanding of how these trends will impact each and every one of us now and in the future. Only by accepting individual accountability will we generate organizational accountability and successful adaptation to these changes. That is our real job in the future. If we can all become more able to adapt at ever-increasing speeds, finding rewarding work will take care of itself!

QUESTIONS FOR REFLECTION

- Reflecting on how these trends will affect you personally in the next ten years, what will be different about jobs in your field or industry?
- Do you currently face issues in attracting and retaining qualified workers, and do you estimate this will get better or worse in the future?
- What would you most like to change about your job, and what does this suggest about staying in your current position, versus changing jobs or careers?

DO'S AND DON'TS

- **Do** design jobs to contain meaning, challenge and accomplishment.
- **Do** remember the concept of "death of the joe job" and how this relates to your workforce.
- **Do** believe the person doing the job knows it best, so get out of the way.

- **Do** consider the broader socio-economic implications of the shrinking labour pool and how this impacts job design and structure in your company.
- **Do not** live by the old employment contract of "jobs for life."
- **Do not** think people will accept jobs that are not interesting and fulfilling in the future.

EXERCISE FOR TEAM LEARNING

In this first paragraph are instructions for a Case Study to be done with your team. Give each person the scenario that follows to go away and work on individually for one week. Then, have team members return to talk about how they would handle the situation below. Distill for yourself the best ideas as part of your own learning about Jobs.

Here is the exercise: you are the general manager of a manufacturing plant that runs around the clock to keep up with demand for your product. There are three shifts per day of eight hours each, with all workers scheduled for two breaks and a lunch period of one-and-a-quarter hours. The plant has been suffering from both declining productivity and high turnover during the past two years. In addition, hiring new workers has increasingly become more difficult and is now averaging eight to ten weeks for each open position. You are worried and not sure what can be done about the problem. The CEO has come to you and offered the following option: either solve the problem within the next six months or the plant will be closed and the work moved offshore to an Asian "Tiger" economy that seems more attractive for the corporation. Your management team is recommending you simply inform employees of the potential loss of their jobs unless productivity improves. You sense the underlying problem will go away with a more creative solution, but are not sure where to begin. The easy choice is always available; however, you decide you should explore alternative solutions. Sit down with a blank piece of paper and make a list of issues you feel would need to be addressed if you are to generate creative solutions and open yourself to new possibilities.

FIRST STEPS ALONG THE WAY

Assigned Task	*Expected Outcome*
If your firm has job descriptions, find three representative 'typical' jobs and read them carefully. Would you be inspired to apply for these positions and committed to doing them well? Why? Why not?	*Develops an awareness of how your firm currently structures work, to determine if you have a potential problem or true possibility.*
Consider if you have a target retirement age, and why. Is it because work prevents you from doing what you really want to do? If work allowed you more freedom and flexibility, think about whether you would keep working longer.	*Unearths how much of our response is caught up in our definitions of what a job represents—control, effort and restrictions, rather than passion, purpose and fulfillment. Could also invite you to reflect upon the impact on society of changing this perception.*

Knowing

> **Intuition becomes increasingly valuable in the new information society precisely because there is so much data.**
>
> —John Naisbitt

We always know. What do you mean, we always 'know'? Think about your own life for a moment. Have you not had times when you knew with inner clarity what course of action you should take in a given situation—even if you did not have all the information you thought you needed? Mind you, you might not necessarily have followed your inner wisdom. If that was the case, what was the consequence of ignoring your knowing? We will wager that many of you regretted going against your instincts. That is because you knew what to do—even if you did not realize it consciously at the time.

What else do we know? We know in our heart of hearts

how we are being in our external interactions, even if we do not always care to admit it. We may find clever ways to justify uncomfortable discrepancies between how we would prefer to see ourselves and how we are actually being. But on some level, we cannot hide from our conscience. Perhaps there are times when you wish you could have stepped away from yourself because you realized your actions were not particularly attractive. We found especially clear evidence of this sense of "knowing on the inside" with one of our coaching clients. We give him enormous credit for facing up to the negative impact of his silent rage when confronted. As soon as we pointed out times when this dynamic had shown up in the workplace, he remembered immediately the minute details. In the example we are referring to, he knew exactly that he was projecting his rage over unresolved issues with some of the people involved by taking it out on more 'innocent' players in the room. He admitted that he knew in the moment what he was doing; he just chose not to alter his behaviours. But there was no doubt he knew the damage he was inflicting.

What else do we know? We know the answers to all our life questions are ultimately on the inside. "*Are they?*" you may ask. Yes, they are—even if you may have lost sight of this truth for whatever reason. As a result of disconnecting from our inner wisdom, many wind up looking outside themselves for solutions, as if others held better or smarter answers. If we dare go within long enough, though, we will always find in the core of our being a sense of knowing why things are happening in our lives, and often, what to do about it. This fact is proven time and time again in our coaching practices. Leaders often ask us what we think they should do to solve a problem, or they ask what we would do in the same situation. Not infrequently, we turn this question back to them to consider it more deeply from the perspective of inner knowing. What we invariably find is that they come up with the answer themselves—an answer far better than we could have necessarily given them, at that.

We think you can start to see for yourself from these scenarios that our inner knowing really does operate all the time. Whether we realize it or not, it has been at play in every decision we have made. However, for many of us, our wisdom operates without our complete awareness. And as long as that is the case, we risk it taking us into situations we would have avoided had we 'known.' Only by bringing to our full attention our inner knowing can we start to harvest its full power. Only by realizing the degree to which our projection of ourselves into the external world actually mirrors our inner world can we start to change behaviours with true choice. Only by understanding more about ourselves are we able to offer more of ourselves to the world.

"But how does all this talk about inner knowing relate to leadership?" you wonder. Let us ask you this: as a leader would you rather "hit and miss" in making business decisions, or would you rather have a set of more reliable techniques you can count on that significantly up your "strike ratio"? We suspect your answer is the latter, not the former.

To begin to apply this content, first realize that inner knowing essentially involves listening to and trusting oneself. If you think about it, these are long-recognized leadership competencies. So, the good news is that you are already on the way! The need for leaders who can create what is not yet known—a future that comes from inner knowing rather than the tried-and-true formulas of yesterday or today—will only increase. As our lives become filled with ever-vaster amounts of data to process (as alluded to by John Naisbitt in our opening quote), the ability to tap into one's inner wisdom will simply become a natural expectation of successful leadership and performance.

Einstein is reported to have said we use only two to ten percent of our ability; imagine how far we could go beyond those figures using inner knowing. Given the dynamic nature of today's world, it only makes sense to cultivate a wisdom-based mindset within organizations. Thinking "outside the box" allows us to see past self-imposed boundaries and thereby create the inspired cultures after which business leaders are always questing.

Interestingly, more and more organizations are expanding their attitudes toward alternative forms of business 'knowing'. To us, this is a very encouraging sign. These workplaces are recognizing that listening to and trusting oneself can be used to solve problems and improve decision-making, ultimately increasing results.

For these reasons, we were heartened by a fascinating example from the Marines. Two gurus were hired to develop a martial arts program combining meditation, centering techniques and mastery of a dozen "warrior values." The program encourages self-awareness and self-exploration—with a focus on gaining a disciplined mind, winning and peace rather than killing. When we read about this, we were surprised—not by the warrior elements, but by the teaching of spiritual practices. The martial arts have long been known as a spiritual teaching ground, but we would have expected the Marines to be the last place where exploration of one's inner world would be taught—let alone promoted! This gives us further hope for the workplace. If the Marines can embrace a different way of being, then we suggest corporations can, too.

Second, to put inner knowing to work for you in an organizational context, simply notice it. Since we have been largely taught to ignore intuitive impressions, we must counteract our conditioning by filtering in—not out—insights that come to our attention from either our internal or external environments. We develop our awareness of these clues by noticing what we are noticing. In effect, this means becoming an observer of your own life. When we are facilitating, we sometimes have participants imagine taking a helicopter ride above the scenery surrounding them; looking down from these heights, they are better able to see what is happening in their lives.

From our experience as coaches, we can attest to the revelations gained when clients are encouraged to notice by turning inward. Let's give an example of the power that noticing our inner world can offer. In that context, we like to say that we possess no answers; our 'only' role is to call forth clients' wisdom through powerful questions and listening. While it almost feels too simplistic, we observe repeatedly that when we hold others in our hearts and minds this way, this is how they 'show up' around us. In other words, whether you hold others as wise and resourceful or not, that is precisely how they will perform around you.

We find this point has interesting applicability for your interactions with direct reports. How many times do they come to you seeking out answers to issues they could resolve themselves? Wouldn't it be great to be able to show them techniques to develop their decision-making? If your answer to these questions is "*yes*," then you understand another aspect of what we are providing in this chapter. Once having understood for yourself a notion like "noticing," there is nothing stopping you from 'teaching' it to others so as to draw out their innate wisdom over time. Talk about a way to extend your reach by having a fully empowered team equipped to think through and solve their own issues. Would that make a difference for you? We think so!

We do recognize that this approach takes some getting used to, because we are conditioned to place our faith in external authority figures rather than being the authorities in our own lives. Again, this is because we have come to believe the answers we seek are somehow "out there" rather than being available to us on the inside.

Third, let's turn to the concept of "intentionality." Defined in the dictionary as "directing one's mind or efforts steadfastly toward a specific aim, purpose or plan," we work with our clients on intention by helping them harness their inherent capacity to bring into being whatever they intend to create in their lives. Again, this belief system is initially counterintuitive to how most of us have been taught. Disconnected from our ability to manifest what we intend to happen in our lives, we internalize messages like, *"Don't you become too big for your britches, young man/lady!"* We forget the hugeness of our ability to create the life we want, and regrettably wind up living the way we think others want it to be for us. As a result, much of our life's work on a personal level becomes about remembering who we really are—powerful creators. This journey can be enormously aided by reconnecting to our inner knowing.

Therefore, we work a lot with leaders to help them focus clearly on what they want to happen (for example, during key meetings and interactions). Through our coaching, we invariably find them reporting back that the very things they intended to happen actually occurred—from the smallest of outcomes to the largest of life goals.

While a big surprise for them, it is no surprise to us! If anything, we encourage our clients to practice strengthening their "intentionality" muscles into all kinds of situations, to reinforce the message about our tremendous untapped ability to create our own reality. One leader we work with has even taken to using a hand signal to tell us when he is focusing with intention on a particular outcome. We get such a kick out of this!

When working with "noticing" or "intentionality" (both manifestations of inner knowing), we suggest you set aside your busy mind's activity (what is sometimes referred to as "monkey mind") and instead turn your attention inward to the wisdom of your body and heart. We typically spend so much time in our heads at work, that it helps to rebalance this overuse of the brain by attending to the messages our bodies constantly give us. This is why the meditative and reflective practices we suggest in "First Steps Along The Way" at the end of this chapter are so important.

We are not saying, however, that our rational side should suddenly be dismissed. Rather, logic and inner knowing should ideally work in unison to make you more effective across the spectrum of your business activity. In summary, we find leaders will increasingly need sophisticated skills to succeed in an uncertain future. Inner knowing is precisely one of the core competencies that will be required for both business and personal success in the Idea Age of the twenty-first century. As a soul-inspiring leader, learning to trust your inner knowing means letting yourself be guided by what lies within you and using that information to serve the greater good of everyone around you.

QUESTIONS FOR REFLECTION

- How can you apply inner wisdom in your professional role as a leader as well as in your personal life?
- What insights have you gained from learning about inner knowing, and how can you apply notions like "noticing" and "intentionality"?
- What are some ways you can encourage others in your organization (direct reports, peers, your leader) to trust their inner sense of authority?

DO'S AND DON'TS

- **Do** view inner knowing as one of the 'new' core leadership competencies of the twenty-first century.
- **Do** notice what you are noticing by becoming an observer in your own life.
- **Do** use logic and inner knowing in tandem.
- **Do** harness the power of "intentionality" to make it work for you.
- **Do not** place your reliance on external authority figures as if they knew more.

EXERCISE FOR TEAM LEARNING

Gather your team together for a mini "training" session on inner knowing. Share with them what you have learned in this chapter—particularly the information on "noticing" and "intentionality." Have a group discussion about how inner knowing shows up for each of your direct reports (whether it is through their sense of seeing, hearing or feeling), and talk about how you can more consciously harness each person's intuitive sense in order to make decisions, plan communications—or any other applications the group can think of.

FIRST STEPS ALONG THE WAY

Assigned Task	Expected Outcome
Learn to meditate—whether through yoga, Tai Chi, Qi-gong, walking or running. The medium does not matter so much as setting aside regular time daily to still your mind. Check in with yourself throughout the day and allow your inner knowing to provide you with information.	*These practices strengthen your ability to pick up information related to your five senses, body and emotions. Encourages you to spend more time with your inner world, to counterbalance the tendency to be outward-focused.*
Read something inspirational each day.	*Starts you thinking about your intentions—the act of directing your mind, heart and efforts in focused and deliberate ways to set forth plans and actions to live purposefully.*
Keep a journal where you record insights about what you notice each day. It does not matter so much what you write, but that you take the time to write. Record any observations you wish and begin to notice what you are noticing.	*Facilitates trusting yourself. Noticing the nature and frequency of your inner knowing helps you become more connected to personal power; you can also use this information to help others reclaim their wisdom.*

Learning

> **Leadership and learning are indispenable to each other.**
> —John F. Kennedy

President Kennedy included these words in a speech given in Dallas in 1963. As truths go, Kennedy's words represent a true nugget of knowledge that must be central in any leader's character: we can always learn and improve, no matter how good we are at something already! Yet, we are astonished by repeated calls to coach senior executives who are involved in having to relearn this essential truth. Why is this and what can we do about it?

Let's start with an easy premise: good leadership requires some element of confidence. Confidence, in turn, often derives from a strong ego presence. When this is balanced with personal insight, empathy and an inclination to learn, ego drives leaders to exude confidence in their vision so others feel compelled and comfortable following. More precisely, a willingness to learn acts to counterbalance one's ego, essentially keeping it under control. In this way, a leader derives the ego's benefit without it reducing effectiveness through unbridled egotism.

When there is a loss of desire to learn and continuously improve, the ego runs amok. Self-assured becomes overly confident and eventually turns to self-importance. This cycle is ultimately destructive. The most recent wave of morally corrupt CEOs and Boards without the self-assurance to rein them in is proof positive of the error of egotism. With ego as the driver, over time a leader's persuasion becomes less personally authentic and more power- or position-centric. This robs them of the true privilege and power of leadership. It reduces them to using derivative authority rather than the more naturally effective persuasion that comes from followers choosing to follow out of moral respect. As a result, the very skills and attitudes that helped them become leaders in the first place are displaced by an egocentric sense of entitlement—as if they deserve to be leaders by virtue of who they are or what they have accomplished. It's almost like a corporate virus, for which we must all seek a cure in order to heal.

As a leader's world begins to unravel, he or she may sense all is not well. More often than not, the leader may have only a vague notion of the real problem. The ego has once again interfered. Only rare individuals can pull themselves out of this steep dive without serious introspection or coaching. All too often, the outcome is a spectacular failure since this is ultimately the only thing that can catch the person's attention. And this is when we get the phone call—from the outplacement firm, from the Board or from the now-tarnished executive who has crashed and burned and is in what we have come to call "ego recovery." Although this is a harsh way for it to occur, this abrupt event often represents the first stage of healing. Rather than being career ending, this can actually become an opportunity to reconstruct an understanding of success by drawing on strengths and repairing weaknesses.

So, what did Kennedy know that so many less-intuitive leaders seem to miss? He knew that the important thing to monitor as a leader was his learning—not his power, not his plan, not even his vision or its execution. What was important, if he was to continue leading, was to continue learning. This simple sentence contains enormous defensive power for any leader. The downward cycle we just described can never befall those who follow this dictum. Embracing this philosophy deeply and personally actually acts like an immune-system booster against an oversized ego. In our experience, the surest way to remain sharp as a leader is to actually seek out opportunities to learn rather than lead, since leadership opportunities are boundless for those who are always learning. Put another way, the higher your calling to lead on an ever-larger scale, the higher your need for continuous learning. Conclusion? Those who are continuous learners really make the best leaders. We call this our "leadership learning paradox."

This concept is derived from basic knowledge management theory and results in a kind of "food chain of knowledge." Each element contains deep insights into learning useful for you as a leader and in helping you judge the real leadership capacity and commitment of your organization. Once understood, the information can be applied in so many situations as a diagnostic tool and to create urgency of action on real leadership issues.

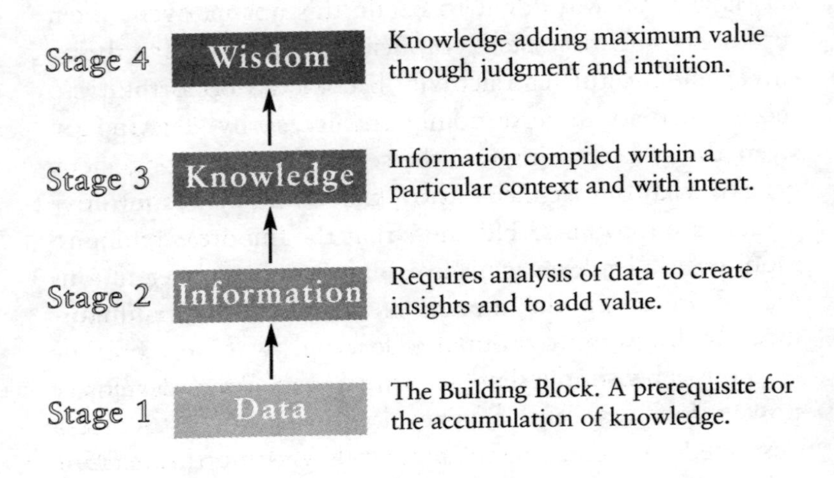

The diagram above indicates how knowledge, and data or information, are not at all the same thing. This is an important distinction, since many leaders are confused and dazzled by the amount of information they receive daily about their organizations. Report after report, memos and e-mails galore fill their in-baskets, all sent by well-intentioned colleagues desperate to share their perspectives on the business. Yet, so much of this information and data is of no real value to the leader. Sent by managers, for whom it may appear to have lots of value, it lacks a context or intent that turns information into knowledge. What do we mean by context or intent? This is what the leader must decide—*in what context or with what intent am I collecting what information?* Information generated at random is only guaranteed to generate random results!

In our consulting roles, we also use this tool to diagnose an organization's maturity. Stage One organizations are generally younger, growing quickly and lucky if they even know what time of day it is, let alone anything about their customers' buying habits, bank balances or other critical management information. Even getting data is often difficult in these organizations. Similarly, when they begin to get past this barrier and mature their information management systems and flows, they are tempted to stop since they now have information rather than just data. They are often quite proud of themselves for this advancement to Stage Two. And so on… until they reach the point of having and consistently using organizational wisdom.

You see, good leaders act with intent. They develop a sense of the issues and immediately seek help to assess options or validate perspectives. They demonstrate their vulnerability and encourage everyone, including themselves, to access sources of learning and knowledge on the topic at hand. Leaders who rely on lower-level information to provide this intent or context risk being manipulated by the information; this is the old "statistics lie" you may have heard about. Without strong confidence in an answer, it is easy to generate a statistic to support virtually any position on just about any issue. As we should now know, that is not what soul-inspiring leadership is about. Smart leaders reject data and information and look for knowledge and wisdom as their guideposts.

Next, let us move on to the more complex question of how you generate wisdom and knowledge from data and information. The basis for this insight is contained in some work done by Ikujiro Nonaka, in which he describes tacit and explicit knowledge. Explicit knowledge is readily observed, collected, stored and shared. A recipe is a good example of explicit knowledge. Tacit knowledge is about the context, culture or convictions required to make use of explicit knowledge appropriately. For instance, tacit knowledge may be the confidence to believe, based on past experience, that you can follow a recipe successfully. Knowledge and wisdom come from the ability to use explicit knowledge in conjunction with tacit knowledge—to put data and information into an appropriate context that enables the information to become more valuable. This form of rational thought and analytic capability—the very ability to reason—is what makes human beings so unique in our world.

In business, this suggests you must learn to understand not only the obvious, but less obvious aspects of how any task is performed in your organization. You must know not just how transactions are processed, but about the delivery of less tangible aspects of customer service derived from employees' commitment and satisfaction levels. This is an example of explicit versus tacit knowledge; you may know how many transactions are being processed per day and at what cost (information), but do you really know how well customers are being treated as these orders are processed (knowledge)? If you do, can you combine these sources to create a better outcome for both customers and your company by improving both the *what* and *how* of transaction processing (wisdom)?

Let us hasten to add that we do not actually believe many of the so-called knowledge management projects underway today in organizations will yield much in terms of long-term ROI. Why? Because most of them come from a perspective of knowledge as an asset of the business, something they want to manage as any other asset. Many of these projects include the notion of trying to extract tacit knowledge from employees' heads into systems that make this knowledge available to others in the firm. While each of these sounds like a laudable goal, each in our view has a fundamental flaw.

Two things of note—one is that any exercise to document tacit knowledge locked in employees' heads assumes that this information will ultimately be useful to someone else. This violates a major premise we have tried to help our clients understand: "*It's about the people!*" While we can extract the knowledge (maybe), what we cannot replicate is the dedication, loyalty, insight and tenacity of a single employee acting in the best interests of the business to see the company's mission accomplished. As we so often say in our speeches, "*Nobody gets out of bed every morning hoping to have a bad day, inflict pain and generally feel like a failure.*" Human beings have a natural desire to achieve results and feel successful—it is organizations and management that often get in the way of this. And, we feel, many knowledge management initiatives risk dehumanizing already toxic work environments that much further by assuming, "*if we could only unlock what it is they know in their heads*"—read the subtext—"*maybe we wouldn't need to rely on them as much or need as many of them.*" This is the wrong approach, and it will not generate the expected results. The smart organizations are those that look to these same dedicated employees to say: "*What kind of knowledge do you need to do your jobs better and how can we help you with knowledge management tools?*" We just do not see any successful projects focused on extracting and documenting tacit knowledge that have yielded any real long-term improvements, and thus we caution against that generally as an approach.

Our second fear is that organizations often apply the term "asset" only to those things perceived to have a dollar value. And this often results in a very financially oriented view about how to manage these assets. If this view is expressed with regard to information, it becomes something to hoard rather than share. Assets need to be protected and audited, for example. This does not build a collaborative model that enhances teamwork and collective wisdom shared among colleagues. Yet this is the very model that we are espousing as being required to succeed in today's hypercompetitive world. So we encourage you to pay close attention to language and to the inherent message you may be sending out about knowledge in your organization; treat knowledge management initiatives as collaborative tools that can help improve your intellectual capital. When this healthier perspective is applied to the challenge of information-overload for individual employees at all levels, you have great potential to derive benefits that matter to your workplace.

And what is the most important benefit to be derived from encouraging organizational learning? It is awareness. While not generally all that easily measured, your organization's ability to sense what is happening first in the environment and then to correctly diagnose the potential opportunities and threats this represents to the business is what drives good organizations to become great. When we combine this awareness with an ability to execute swiftly, you build a capability we call "organizational agility." Since we are so often challenged to quantify the benefits of these kinds of soft-skills, especially when dealing with the financial side of the house, we have developed a very simple equation that sometimes helps our clients:

SIMPLE LEADERSHIP EQUATION #4:

Organizational Agility = Quality of Insight + Speed of Execution

To quantify the benefits of agility for any organization, you need only think about the true accrued value of improving the quality of strategic insights. What would it be worth to your organization to improve, just marginally, decision-making at every level and focus it on your competitive domain? And, if you could improve learning about how to execute tasks more quickly and efficiently, would that be worth something to you? Our limited view of the world today suggests that the essence of "competitive advantage" (and we use the term quite loosely, recognizing that many readers may work in the public or not-for-profit sectors where this term needs to be read in context and modified to suit your particular mission) rests almost exclusively on the concept of improving "time-to-market." This is an organization's ability to quickly realize value through bringing tangible products and services to market that are innovative and meet customer needs literally just in time. This can only be accomplished through an improvement in organizational agility.

Let us finally talk about another point of intrigue: in many organizations we deal with, knowledge management has ended up being confused with information technology or placed under the IT or systems group. Often, knowledge management is thought of as some kind of "data warehouse" project. Now, from a technologist's perspective, we believe this is an excellent technology that may be appropriate to many organizations. However, let us not confuse the collection and storage of data centrally (the essence of a data warehouse project) with any of the more sophisticated concepts we have just been exploring. While database management tools and techniques are powerful enablers of any knowledge management strategy, leaders must first recognize the obligation to have a successful business strategy that includes learning and knowledge management as key components. Then, they need to challenge their IT groups to rise to the occasion by playing a fundamental role in linking the IT-enabling strategy to this emerging business strategy. It cannot successfully play out the other way. You must avoid the easy trap of basing your learning strategy on what IT recommends you do with your data assets!

So, learning is key. As a leader, you must always be seeking to grow through learning. This is of personal benefit to you. You must then breed a culture of awareness in your organization that encourages learning at all levels, enabling "organizational agility." This is of tangible benefit to your organization, because this key strategy builds sustainable long-term competitive advantage for your organization. Any questions?

QUESTIONS FOR REFLECTION

- When was the last time you focused on learning something completely new, and what was the subject?
- What is it like for you to learn? (e.g., invigorating, rewarding, challenging, etc.)
- Answer the question: "If I could only completely learn about one thing, it would be..."

DO'S AND DON'TS

- **Do** keep in mind the "leadership learning paradox" that states the higher your calling to lead, the higher your need for continuous learning.
- **Do** use the "food chain of knowledge" to judge the real leadership capacity and commitment of your organization.
- **Do** distinguish explicit and tacit knowledge, knowing wisdom comes from putting data and information into a context that makes the information valuable.
- **Do not** let your ego run amok through unwillingness to learn.
- **Do not** confuse knowledge and data or information as being the same thing.

EXERCISE FOR TEAM LEARNING

Ask for volunteers from your team to help you review your organization's training and development practices. Although formal training is one element of learning, it is often the least effective. Determine if your practices are current and whether they make use of a variety of learning strategies, such as self-study, coaching, mentoring, cross training and knowledge systems. Look at how you can take advantage of methodologies that are not presently supported. Build an ROI-based case for what your team comes up with and present it to senior management. Implement the ideas by making sure you have a specific time-based training and development plan for each member of your team.

FIRST STEPS ALONG THE WAY

Assigned Task	*Expected Outcome*
Find two books about knowledge management with which you are not familiar and read them thoroughly. Seek to understand the basics and apply them to your organization as you read.	*Begin to understand the power of knowledge versus information and how to create systems and processes that are knowledge-enabled. Understanding and applying these concepts diligently promotes action learning within your organization and improves results.*
Establish a personal learning plan with a time span of 2–5 years. Identify major skill or knowledge areas you feel would benefit you.	*Empowers control of your own learning and improves your abilities over time. Demonstrates role-model leadership concerning continuous learning and improvement.*

Maturity

> Until you make peace with who you are, you will never be content with what you have.
>
> —Doris Mortman

In our travels speaking, consulting to organizations and coaching individuals, we are often struck by how much the world expects conformity as the "socially correct" behaviour that will take you farthest in life. Yet, emotional and spiritual maturity probably requires just the opposite reaction. If we are truly to be "at peace with ourselves" we propose the radical thought that this actually requires a different code of conduct than what we may have been taught growing up.

This may tempt you to make a connection between being a bit of a rebel and the ability to achieve emotional and spiritual maturity. That is not what we are suggesting. Nor are we equating maturity with age or experience, for we have both known many who were young and very wise as well as those who were old and foolish. Rather, we are linking emotional and spiritual maturity to a certain comfort with who you are on the inside rather than always worrying about what those around you are thinking, or projecting the consequences of your own behaviour on others because it is too difficult to take responsibility for yourself.

As such, there are for us three general elements that define maturity, for they show up consistently in those we admire for their emotional and spiritual achievements. These three vital sources of maturity are:

- Resolve any unresolved past;
- Become comfortable inside your own skin;
- Make your own happiness the number one priority.

We propose all three of these as "non-negotiables." We have found you cannot achieve a true state of maturity through depth and accomplishment in only one of these areas. Based on our years of being in private coaching practice, it is only through systematically achieving all three outcomes that one arrives at a state of emotional and spiritual maturity. Modifying the words somewhat, but not the intent, we have reduced this critical self-development concept to a fairly simple equation as we have done elsewhere in our book:

SIMPLE LEADERSHIP EQUATION #5:

Maturity = Resolution + Peace + Joy

We also believe that this can be a temporary state: at any point in time, you may be OK with all three or in crisis with all three or some mix therein. You may find for a period of time that everything in one area is fine, yet another area will take an enormous amount of energy to sort out. Everyone is different in this respect and no two people will ever come to this process in the same way. So we leave up to you how you journey down this path, but we do encourage you to run (or at least pick up the pace a little!) and get there sooner rather than later, so that you can ensure you lead a happy and rewarding, soul-inspiring life.

Let us take each of the elements of our equation in order. We subscribe to the theory, and see it in practice, that you must first resolve anything from your past that is unresolved for you. This is not about anybody else, but rather about something that is impacting you. To put it into the realm of psychology, what traces of your past from your family life, upbringing, sibling relationships, past marriages or any other kind of experience have not been fully integrated for you? For every bad experience there is still a positive lesson to take away, but there is a need to forgive and move on. So, who have you not forgiven for sins in the past? What is still preventing you from putting the past into perspective and moving into the future confident that you have mastered your own emotional and spiritual context? Any and all of these issues, which are pressing and even depressing for many people, must be long resolved in order to achieve a state of emotional and spiritual maturity.

Now, we are not naïvely suggesting there won't always be issues that arise time and time again for you, that there will not be emotional crises in the future. Rather, it is the ability to let go of negative experiences in our lives (and not hang onto them) which defines the ability to be at peace with our past. Each lesson in life, no matter how hard won, must be seen as only that—a lesson. And a lesson must be learned. Once it's learned, you are able to avoid repeating the mistakes in your past and move instead confidently into the future.

Now that we know something about what "at peace with the past" looks and feels like, let's examine the opposite of this aspect of emotional and spiritual maturity through a story. It is about a leader's failure to shine the spotlight on her own unresolved family-of-origin issues, thereby triggering a chain of negative reactions across her entire department.

In our coaching, we often talk about holding up "the mirror of examination" to our actions, with the objective of encouraging clients to take full accountability for their impact on others. In the case of this dysfunctional vice-president, we discovered a fascinating interpretation of the mirror. Normally, when we sit across from someone examining their actions in a 'mirror,' the reflective surface is facing toward them. Not so with Vicky. While staunchly claiming to take responsibility for her actions, she invariably managed to manipulate so-called learning dialogues into twisted psychological exercises that left others almost destroyed and herself seemingly unscathed. It was always the other person's fault. Vicky, on the other hand, obliviously went about her daily routine in the deluded belief that if it were not for her efforts to 'fix' others, things would be a disaster.

Like a two-faced Madonna, she enticed her direct reports to reveal to her their deepest hopes and fears, but not to build trusting relationships as do soul-inspiring leaders. No, her only objective was to use this information against people later on. Yes, Vicky would carry the façade of showing her true self, but only enough to trick others into revealing their true thoughts and feelings, again for ammunition down the road. Unlike skilled leaders who make it safe for team members to examine their strengths and areas of opportunity, "developmental dialogues" with Vicky became wounding 'opportunities' that belittled and devastated. To say there are people who reported to her over ten years ago still wearing tread marks across their backs is no exaggeration. Such deplorable abuse of power by a leader obviously represents for us the antithesis of soul-inspiring leadership.

Rather than take responsibility for examining and transforming her own limiting beliefs, she focused singularly on others' limits as she saw them. Rather than acknowledge she was recreating in the workplace the family dynamic in which she had grown up, she labeled everyone else as messed up. Hers was an abject failure to realize that one finger pointing toward others meant three fingers were pointing in her direction. Never once was there the consideration: "*What are those three fingers pointing to in me?*"

Our second principle of emotional and spiritual maturity, "being comfortable inside your own skin," is for us a result of investing the time and energy to conquer our own personal 'demons' and thereby actually arrive at a place of enjoying our own company. We find that by cultivating awareness of their own souls, leaders start to earn the right to be called mature. In truth, one cannot ask others to travel to places one is not first prepared to journey oneself.

Being willing to travel through one's inner territory is a courageous journey that demands much soul searching. On the other side of such inward reflection lies enormous reward. Rather than always wanting to run away from ourselves, we become our own best friends. Rather than projecting our 'stuff' onto others, we own it. Rather than unquestioningly accepting others' opinions about how to live our lives, we go by what is right for us, trusting our inner counsel.

Only by setting aside regular doses of quiet time do we feel leaders can achieve such comfort from the inside out. Through our coaching practices, we find introspection is often heightened in people's lives by crisis-related events like employment termination, illness, accidents or death of a loved one. While we do not wish catastrophe upon anyone, we find crisis has a way of propelling real growth—providing we are open to the hidden opportunity. But why wait for an emergency? Why not make it easier on yourself by engaging in regular quiet time that connects you to your inner core? Not navel-gazing, but connecting to who you really are so you can lead from that perspective in the outer world.

In this way, there is also a relationship between "at peace with the past" and "being comfortable inside your own skin." Mature leaders have compassion for the reality of most people's upbringings, realizing that we learn at an early age to shape our behaviours in order to gain privileges and approval. Many of us never escape this part of our past and go on acquiring personas of various ilks: professional, personal and others. Recognizing through their own personal growth work that these identities often have little in common with who we are at our core, mature leaders use learning acquired through therapeutic or other interventions—not to promote themselves as counselors (dangerous!), but rather to share how they have come to terms with their own lives. Interested fundamentally in seeing others blossom into their greatness, their service in this context is about making a difference in others' lives by helping them be at peace and comfortable inside of themselves, too. Engaged at an appropriate level of intimacy with others, mature leaders are truly able to share themselves and support others in seeking their own true selves.

The last of our three maturity imperatives rests on coming to appreciate that a definition of a full life must include making yourself happy. We find it ultimately ironic that by being what others might call self-indulgent in this regard, we are actually able to put our best foot forward and make others happy. In the airline industry, this is about putting on your own oxygen mask first in a travel emergency, so that you can in fact help other passengers. After all, you can be of no service if you are dead! We say, if this premise is logically accepted on airplanes, then why can it not be applied to other areas of life?

In our personal coaching, we use a term called "extreme self care," which essentially means to care for one's self so that one can continue to give to others. Our clients at first tend to confuse this notion with selfishness, which it is not. Instead of creating a sure recipe for resentment by looking after others and ignoring their own needs, mature leaders know everyone wins when they keep themselves in their own life's picture, so to speak. This includes, amongst other things, keeping appropriate boundaries around their time and relationships at work, so that they do not sacrifice what brings them happiness in life in the name of work. While extensively covered in the chapter on Balance, this idea bears repeating here, for it is such a key premise of our book.

In conclusion, we believe you will agree with us that emotional and spiritual maturity has much to do with personal mastery. For soul-inspiring leaders, it is synonymous with a way of being that continuously asks: "*Is this how I want to live my life? Is this how I want to be treated or treat others?*" All actions are scrutinized to ensure they reflect "at peace with their past," "comfortable inside one's skin" and "brings happiness." There is no choice but to turn toward, not away from, spirit. Those who choose maturity will reap its consequential reward. Those who choose immaturity will equally get what they deserve.

QUESTIONS FOR REFLECTION

- What is present for you about your family and your past that may still be interfering with your success as a fully integrated, mature adult?
- To what degree are you comfortable inside your own skin, and what changes would you like to make to this aspect of your maturity?
- How do you choose to interpret the notion "extreme self-care"—as self-caring or selfish? What does that tell you?

DO'S AND DON'TS

- **Do** hold up "the mirror of examination" to your life, in order to take full responsibility for the impact of your own actions.
- **Do** see negative past experiences as lessons to be learned; move on and use them to your benefit in the future.
- **Do** learn to enjoy your own company and treat yourself as an ally.
- **Do** recognize that the definition of a full life must include making yourself happy.
- **Do not** equate emotional and spiritual maturity with age or experience.
- **Do not** find others to blame for the state of your life.

EXERCISE FOR TEAM LEARNING

We often show up for others most authentically in our behaviours and emotional responses. To help you access more of your innermost thoughts and feelings, meet with three people who know you very well. Ask them to respond honestly and without fear of repercussion to the following question: "*What do you think it would be like to live in my shoes?*" When answering, remind them to set aside their assumptions and viewpoints, based on what they know about you. Now, ask three colleagues or team members the same thing. Note any differences between the two groups—acute differences may indicate a failure to show your true self to others consistently. Finally, on a scale of one percent (*hardly accomplished*) to one hundred percent (*fully accomplished*), how would each of these people rate you in the three areas we have outlined that are prerequisites to emotional maturity? Make sure you understand why they rated you the way they did and then compare this to your self-assessment. How can this exercise contribute to greater self-awareness on your way towards full emotional maturity?

FIRST STEPS ALONG THE WAY

Assigned Task	*Expected Outcome*
Identify any people from your past (family, friends, teachers, former colleagues) with whom you still have outstanding issues. Determine that you will get 'complete' (i.e., resolved) with them by a self-imposed deadline in each case. Your completion process could take a number of forms—in person, by phone, in writing, in your own mind without any direct conversation at all.	*Brings resolution to this part of your life and frees up energy that has been invested (all these years) in staying connected to them through negativity. Makes you more available and present to those who are in your life today.*
Create a monthly schedule whereby you spend blocks of time only with yourself. This schedule should include, at minimum, a lengthier 'date' with yourself on weekend time and at least one evening per week that contains even a short block of time alone.	*Encourages regular introspection time in order to increase your degree of comfort inside your own skin. Ultimately results in you enjoying your own company and gaining other benefits that come from this time just for yourself.*

Assigned Task	*Expected Outcome*
Brainstorm a list of at least ten items that for you would define "extreme self care." The list can contain simple items like going for a walk at lunch hour. Let your imagination take you where it wants to go! Just make sure as many as possible could fit inside the course of a day.	*Considering what actions you would define as caring toward yourself starts to make you conscious of your own needs for support. Writing down your list of ten and posting it somewhere visible keeps reminding you to make regular daily time for "extreme self care."*

Nurturing

> Women have for centuries been recognized as talented listeners, nurturers, motivators, communicators. These very qualities that we once were told were unbusinesslike are precisely the qualities that business needs most to tap human potential.
>
> —Mary Cunningham Agee

In reading this chapter's quote, have you concluded this is another manifesto railing against injustices experienced by women in the workplace? If so, let us ease this concern. In speaking of nurturing, we are no more suggesting men should become like women any more than it has made sense for women to emulate men. If there were an injustice against which we *do* rail, it is the unfairness of being expected to shelve parts of ourselves while at work—nurturing or otherwise. For men, it takes the form of denying their feminine qualities for fear of being branded "unmanly." For women, it becomes about squelching so-called masculine traits for fear of being labeled "aggressive."

Such devaluation has created deep divides between the sexes—at work and on a societal level. To heal this unhealthy dynamic, workplaces must become integrated. Segregation must be replaced with connection. In the integrated workplace, men and women offer their inherent strengths to one another, growing and learning as a result of this valuable exposure.

On an individual or personal level, we define integration as "internal alignment." In our experience, coaching and mentoring (while different) are prime examples of the need for this internal cooperation between our so-called masculine and feminine traits. We each possess both sets—often in varying proportions, with a preference for one over the other. To be an effective coach or mentor, we are ideally able to balance both masculine and feminine qualities; they work hand in glove.

For example, mentors do a lot of supporting—an activity that often comes more easily to women, who are not as conditioned to see support as indulgent. Equally, mentors must challenge their protégés and deliver difficult feedback—skills typically developed in men, trained not to shy away from imposing their own viewpoint. When we establish coaching contracts with our leader-clients, we include an explicit agreement as to how trust will be safeguarded in our relationship; we find safety to be a foundational value for many women. At the same time, coaching demands utmost openness and honesty—qualities facilitated by men's need for independence. These are just some ways both nurturing feminine qualities and provocative masculine traits are given space in the developmental dialogue between mentors/coaches and leaders.

At the same time, we have read accounts of leaders who believe nurturing others is mutually exclusive from getting on with business. For them, nurturing is merely an underhanded way to support longer working hours while doing nothing to reduce inhumane workloads.

As with many matters leadership-related, we must come back to motive. If leaders are nurturing their workforce solely to wrench more output per employee, then this "churn and burn" attitude must be stringently questioned. If a leader's voice speaks kindness while his or her actions feel punishing, such misalignment must inevitably show up on the bottom line through absenteeism, turnover and low productivity.

Let us at this point share several actual cases from our consulting experience to bring these distinctions alive. Our first example involves an employee initially dismissed for her nurturing ways. Ultimately, the story became a lesson for her colleagues in achieving results while standing true to one's compassionate self. At the start, Ellen was constantly belittled through snide remarks from both her immediate supervisor and their leader for being too 'soft.' She was even told she would have to go on a developmental (read performance improvement) plan in order to "make the tough decisions" in interactions with others. There were no performance issues to speak of, only perceptions. Ironically, this scenario took place inside a human resources department! But then again, we submit that destructive human resources departments are neither staffed by "humans" nor are they a "resource"!

So, what was the underlying issue? Surely there must have been more to it than being too nurturing? Not really.

It seems all the employees outside Ellen's team recognized her as the only HR person who answered their questions with understanding; they only wanted to deal with her. Ellen was also the only HR team member willingly invited to parties for departing and retiring employees. Everyone knew and loved Ellen for her nurturing ways, except her envious teammates. Despite the negative spin her boss cast upon this professional's relating style, she accomplished what she needed to in very effective ways. It is clear to us that the aggressive approaches her leaders tried to foist on her would have actually had the opposite effect. In fact, Ellen's soft-yet-strong negotiating style saved the company significant sums of money in the processing of difficult benefits claims. In the end, one of her two leaders finally conceded they could learn something from her by declaring: "*Maybe we've given you too hard a time. We could probably learn something from how you handle these situations.*" Looks like it dawned on them that they might just catch more flies with honey than vinegar!

The other examples involve men who were highly attuned to the nurturing power of food. In one organization, the leader-director placed great value on regularly making his home available for team get-togethers. Opening his home was a symbolic gesture akin to opening his heart. His nurturing intentions were tangible in the atmosphere created and the loving way he prepared and presented his tantalizing meals. In the second workplace, on a very tiring day of cold-call blitzing, the firm's senior partner cooked up a storm in order to serve sales vice-presidents a full gourmet meal. He took great joy in precisely crafting his fabulous concoctions, all with a pure attitude of caring.

The common theme is one of thoughtfulness—leaders taking time to think about what would be nurturing for others and putting effort into making their offerings special. The vehicle matters not so much as the thought itself. Whether you bring in donuts for the office, treat people to special lunch gatherings or catered breaks, buy them tickets to events, weekend getaways, dinner or evening on the town, spa visits or weekend retreats, sponsor attendance at outside seminars, or give them an afternoon off to go to a garden show or the beach, what counts is the spirit behind the action. Clearly, soul-inspiring leaders base their actions in such questions as, "*What can I do to make sure these people never forget how much they mean to us?*" Imagine what would be possible in your workplace if you kept that question as a constant guiding motive for your actions.

Nurturing leaders also use whatever resources are at their disposal to transform employees' experience of how much caring exists for them as human beings. Pause for a moment to take in the notion of caring for employees, first as human beings and not first as people on your payroll. When you interact from that mindset, it is an entirely different perspective. And, make no mistake—people feel it "in their bones" when you relate to them from this nurturing viewpoint. Far beyond management by walking around, nurturing is about seeking first to understand what has meaning for others before expecting them to nurture your needs as a leader. Based in spiritual principles, it is caring founded on a profound desire to be of service to others rather than demanding they serve you.

If the organizational family were likened to an actual family, we would see the benefits of having available a variety of positive role models—nurturing and challenging, confronting and caring. All are important to the full development of individuals who work inside the environment.

If you still require a business argument to support rebalancing between masculine and feminine perspectives, let us examine the realities of a global and diverse twenty-first century workplace. We argue this next century will demand that leaders adopt a participative outlook if they are to survive. This will mean tolerating differing viewpoints in making decisions, using cooperative approaches to get work done and generating support by nurturing (not manipulating) others.

As Einstein so eloquently put it, "*No problem can be solved from the same consciousness that created it. We must learn to see the world anew.*" Therefore, let us no longer resort to false distinctions that create painful separation and alienation. Instead, let us appreciate all qualities within ourselves and others. In this way, we balance not only our inner spirit as leaders, but by extension, the organizational and societal soul.

QUESTIONS FOR REFLECTION

- How do our descriptions of masculine and feminine qualities show up in your workplace and in you?
- How could you develop more of those aspects of the masculine or feminine representing your least-preferred style?
- When was the last time you did something 'nurturing' for your team members and/or for yourself?

DO'S AND DON'TS

- **Do** increase your internal alignment by integrating masculine and feminine traits inside yourself.
- **Do** adopt an attitude of thoughtfulness in considering what would be nurturing for others; put effort into making your offerings special.
- **Do** use nurturing as a way to transform employees' experience of how much caring exists for them as human beings.
- **Do not** allow segregation and separation in your workplace.
- **Do not** fall into the "churn and burn" trap.
- **Do not** nurture employees simply to gain more output per person.

EXERCISE FOR TEAM LEARNING

At an upcoming team meeting, leave people with the question of what actions/behaviours they would consider nurturing according to their own definitions. Give them a week to brainstorm ideas and have each person share their list at the following meeting. As a group, talk about the themes and patterns they notice (commonalities, differences). Besides taking these ideas into your own leadership practices with each individual, challenge everyone to use what they have learned to be more consciously nurturing toward their team members.

core, mature leaders use learning acquired through therapeutic or other interventions—not to promote themselves as counselors (dangerous!), but rather to share how they have come to terms with their own lives. Interested fundamentally in seeing others blossom into their greatness, their service in this context is about making a difference in others' lives by helping them be at peace and comfortable inside of themselves, too. Engaged at an appropriate level of intimacy with others, mature leaders are truly able to share themselves and support others in seeking their own true selves.

The last of our three maturity imperatives rests on coming to appreciate that a definition of a full life must include making yourself happy. We find it ultimately ironic that by being what others might call self-indulgent in this regard, we are actually able to put our best foot forward and make others happy. In the airline industry, this is about putting on your own oxygen mask first in a travel emergency, so that you can in fact help other passengers. After all, you can be of no service if you are dead! We say, if this premise is logically accepted on airplanes, then why can it not be applied to other areas of life?

In our personal coaching, we use a term called "extreme self care," which essentially means to care for one's self so that one can continue to give to others. Our clients at first tend to confuse this notion with selfishness, which it is not. Instead of creating a sure recipe for resentment by looking after others and ignoring their own needs, mature leaders know everyone wins when they keep themselves in their own life's picture, so to speak. This includes, amongst other things, keeping appropriate boundaries around their time and relationships at work, so that they do not sacrifice what brings them happiness in life in the name of work. While extensively covered in the chapter on Balance, this idea bears repeating here, for it is such a key premise of our book.

In conclusion, we believe you will agree with us that emotional and spiritual maturity has much to do with personal mastery. For soul-inspiring leaders, it is synonymous with a way of being that continuously asks: "*Is this how I want to live my life? Is this how I want to be treated or treat others?*" All actions are scrutinized to ensure they reflect "at peace with their past," "comfortable inside one's skin" and "brings happiness." There is no choice but to turn toward, not away from, spirit. Those who choose maturity will reap its consequential reward. Those who choose immaturity will equally get what they deserve.

QUESTIONS FOR REFLECTION

- What is present for you about your family and your past that may still be interfering with your success as a fully integrated, mature adult?
- To what degree are you comfortable inside your own skin, and what changes would you like to make to this aspect of your maturity?
- How do you choose to interpret the notion "extreme self-care"—as self-caring or selfish? What does that tell you?

FIRST STEPS ALONG THE WAY

Assigned Task	*Expected Outcome*
Start a file of nurturing ideas on your computer or in a portable journal. You might also carry around a few extra coupons for a free drink at the local coffee or juice shop so you can give them out 'spontaneously.'	*Writing them down becomes a tool for remembering good ideas. Keeping your eyes and ears open for opportunities focuses your search and constantly adds to ways you can nurture those you lead.*
Consider providing oases of renewal in your workplace. This could be as simple as providing a common lounge area for breaks, or it could be a more elaborate separate room set up for relaxation and calming activities.	*Encourages employees to pay attention to their own needs for nurturing. Suggests the organization sponsors and endorses the need to renew throughout the workday.*

Obsolescence

> **The measure of success is not whether you have a tough problem to deal with, but whether it is the problem you had last year.**
>
> —John F. Dulles

During our years as consultants to management, one consistent difference between leaders and managers has emerged. Leaders are constantly aware of the need for change and innovation—they embrace it as a challenge. Prototypical managers, on the other hand, constantly attempt to perpetuate the status quo. This intrinsic difference matters, particularly when you come to realize most of what we understand about the world of work today is based on obsolete thinking.

This awareness of, and ability to accept, change is a competitive advantage soul-inspiring leaders naturally embrace and exhibit... unlike the leadership behaviours inside one long-established firm at which we once worked. Suffering from what we call the "Not Invented Here" syndrome, this company magically believed competition knocked on everyone else's door but their own. Continuous change, quality improvement and operational excellence may have been fine for others, but not needed here! So much of the daily dynamic had to do with maintaining a certain management style—a style rooted in the ways of fifty years earlier and essentially disinterested in the invigorating ideas of younger leaders. Exciting, future-oriented initiatives would be launched with panache, only to fall by the wayside scant months later. Complacent to the point of being lulled into a marketplace stupor, senior management falsely relied on one product line that had carried the organization through decades of near-monopoly-engendered success.

Now living outside their walls, we actually wonder if the danger signals did not start long before the company was rudely awakened from its drowsiness by a double-digit decline rather than an increase in its core market share by an Internet-interloper. Apparently, the degree of its own obsolescence did not strike this firm until its very bread and butter was at risk—long after inroads into other marketplaces had failed miserably because of management's tenacious hold on the old ways. Ours is a tale of the huge cost of complacency and false security. What may have carried them in the early years lacks sufficiency under the scrutiny of new benchmarks and current thinking, and only serves to eradicate shareholder wealth, by the way.

Not that we are without empathy for this organization's plight. We recognize most humans value the status quo to a certain extent and do not always want to see it changed. Let us illustrate by way of personal example. While not perfectly correlated to behaviour, there are certain innate characteristics most people exhibit. One is your handedness; for most of us right, and for some, left. For a very few, it is an almost equal ability to use both. Get up and go into the bathroom, no matter what you are actually doing right now. Think about your morning routine: brushing your teeth, combing your hair, shaving, putting on makeup, scents, gels and creams. Run through this routine exactly as you normally would, but do it all with the hand opposite to the one you would normally use. No matter what, you will find yourself uncomfortable, likely uncoordinated and maybe even incapable of executing this task sufficiently well with your opposite hand. Even if you are ambidextrous, you still have preferences for various activities with one hand over the other; using the other hand provokes some difficulty. Now, with relief that should be palpable to you, resume the routine with your correct hand. You have returned to the 'status quo' and all is now well in your world once more.

While a simple example, this is what organizations often ask of us—quickly learn to do something new, with new tools or approaches, letting the way we have done it for years go by the wayside without even so much as a backward glance. There is no way to give people the comfort of knowing you can return to the status quo, because you cannot—or else as an organization you likely would not have undertaken the change to begin with. Every new initiative seems to scream: "*Get with the program now or we will perish. This change must be accomplished, you will be called upon to do it, and do it with agility*." This is what experts call the "change imperative." And those that do not get with the program risk obsolescence—like the company we described earlier and that we are sure has parallels in your own experience.

We are not judging this phenomenon, for it cannot be practically avoided. Business environments change constantly. Competitiveness calls us to action to constantly improve our quality, costs and revenues. It is never-ending and any leader in any position of influence could share specifically with you the likely consequences of not keeping up with the competitive Joneses!

The call to action, for leaders and followers, is to become adept at creating acceptance of a newly revised version of the status quo. Mentally we need to move from a model of reliance on stability as giving us comfort to a place where our ability to accept and implement change, with control over how that happens, gives us the comfort and security we need to feel less anxious about change.

We therefore propose a new definition of the status quo. It's what we choose to make of it. The status quo is an invention of our own perceptions of what it should be. It should be just like it is, right? Anything else is too scary. Yet, if we injured the hand that we used most frequently, could we learn to do basic tasks with our other hand? Most of us could. And, if we were permanently without our preferred hand, could we eventually make do and even learn to do the tasks as well or better than before? Of course we could. When we are forced to, we embrace the need to change and adapt. Otherwise, we opt for the status quo and just do it the way we always have.

If we learn within our organizations to change the status quo from "the ways things are around here" to "the way we want things to be around here," and we take on a sense of empowerment about our ability to make things the way we want them to be rather than the way they are, we will change our view of change! Suddenly, change becomes an empowering and useful tool to achieve what we want our world to be. Think of it as being completely in control of the status quo, regardless of how it compares to the past. This should help reduce the anxiety many of us associate with change, and instead have us accept change as a fact of life. Instead of being scary, it is an opportunity. There is nothing preventing us from creating what we want, since the way it is now is no longer the massive consideration it once was.

So much of what we have learned, working both within and consulting to organizations and their leaders, has to do with helping others master their environment. We recommend against promising stability, instead providing a context in which people can understand and deal with change in a proactive and productive manner. Honesty about the real state of affairs is ultimately more important than the false sense of security that so often accompanies those who try to shield employees during times of change.

With your interest in our book, we assume you have already concluded our current models of how work gets done are outdated. As a society, we need to rapidly unlearn them if we are to be successful in future. We must begin by acknowledging that current thinking is obsolete.

If you want to truly inspire your soul, think in terms of future possibilities rather than past practices. Embrace change as a permanent state of hypercreativity, where you get to use your skills and abilities to create new opportunities, and then lead others to that same place. When that happens, the real work of your job will be done! To help you move bravely into this future, we can assure you of one thing: unleashing true "people power" is the only path to the future that will make work 'work'! Everything else is truly obsolete.

QUESTIONS FOR REFLECTION

- What makes you anxious about change, and how can you avoid this automatic "fight or flight" human response in the future?
- What is one immediate and constructive thing you could do to improve your organization's ability to embrace change constructively?
- What are the most potent skills you can use to help others learn to thrive, rather than merely survive, during times of intense change?

DO'S AND DON'TS

- **Do** be willing to think anew about your industry/profession.
- **Do** adopt a new definition of the status quo, as "what we choose to make of it."
- **Do** see change as an empowering and useful tool to achieve what you want your world to be.
- **Do not** close down to the idea that your current thinking is obsolete.
- **Do not** rely on stability to give you comfort; instead, adopt a mindset where the ability to accept and implement change provides a sense of 'security.'

- Do not fall prey to the "Not Invented Here" syndrome, as if competition could not come knocking on your door.

EXERCISE FOR TEAM LEARNING

Devote a series of team meetings to examining the degree of obsolescence/complacency in your group and organization. Start by brainstorming ways your thinking and behaviours (as a team and as a workplace) are obsolete versus current. Categorize the 'obsolescence' lists into aspects over which you have direct control, some influence, or no control. Develop action plans to shift items that are under your direct control or over which you have some influence. Establish subgroups of volunteers to see these action plans through to implementation. Have everyone regularly report on progress during subsequent team meetings, and bring your successes to the attention of the senior management team!

FIRST STEPS ALONG THE WAY

Assigned Task	*Expected Outcome*
Formulate three probing questions that can help you determine if an organization is dealing appropriately with the speed of obsolescence in their industry/profession.	*Answering these questions first for yourself gives you some awareness of the problem. Next, bringing this information to an upcoming leadership team meeting adds others' thinking to the mix. It opens up broader dialogue about ways you are vulnerable to obsolescence and generates actions to address these areas of complacency.*
Make a deliberate change in your life that you have wanted to make for some time, but have been afraid to.	*Increases your ability to be proactive about personal change and get comfortable with making change happen rather than waiting for it to happen.*

Passion

> The great leaders are like the best conductors—they reach beyond the notes to reach the magic in the players.
>
> —Blaine Lee

Most organizations operate at suboptimal levels of passion. This should be clear to you when you have witnessed someone in action with true passion for what they do versus those who are simply "at work." In this situation, 'passion' and its associated energy are replaced with 'passive' acceptance of the assigned task. It is sad to encounter so many individuals whose passion stems completely from activities outside of work—perhaps personal causes, hobbies or other associations—given the amount of time they spend working.

One typical means we use to initially diagnose the level of passion in an organization is through "atmosphere."

Since we think of passion as a form of energy, we pick up so much about energy, passion and atmosphere just by paying attention to feelings as we look about public places like lobbies and reception areas, and by observing people's informal interactions.

If you have spent as much time in reception areas as we have, you will know what we mean! Contrast for a moment the somber quality of a front desk bespeaking a staid workplace, where people are discouraged from being loud or otherwise 'inappropriate,' with the vibrant and eclectic décor of a lobby where employees and visitors alike relish chatting with the receptionist because of her energetic presence. Both examples are real. We are sure you can also guess each organization's effects on employees' souls. Expecting people to speak and behave in hushed tones drains one's life force. It crushes spirits and turns human beings into walking automatons. Inviting passion makes people come alive and has them stride about with unbridled energy and purpose. Where would you rather spend half your life?

We find soul-inspiring leaders possess a unique ability to tap into this energy potential and draw it out from stakeholders, employees and customers alike. This elusive quality marks for us the contrast between almost boundless opportunity and the constrained thinking that inhibits people, eliciting only a portion of their energy. It really is the difference between being "at work" and "working at" something!

An example of this passion is evidenced by retailers who create near-religious zeal for their products and services among an intensely loyal following of customers. In turn, overwhelming commitment from sales staff feeds customers' delight as these professionals present their deep product knowledge with obvious energy and passion. When this magical mix occurs, financial returns always follow and shareholders become passionate advocates for the stock, supporting the company with additional capital flows. The passion is evident to all and on display all the time.

Contrast this experience with the last time you visited a department store. Sure, they probably had what you were looking for. And the service was adequate. But there seems to be a missing spark in these encounters. It is not that the clerk isn't friendly; it is just that the person is not passionate about what he or she does. He simply does what is expected and expects you to do the same. If they have what you want, he will sell it to you and if not, he will wish you a nice day and move on to the next customer. We have all experienced this difference, and we intuitively sense it in our response to exceptional encounters.

What, then, do winning organizations do that others do not? How can we become more passionate about what we do? For without passion, there can only be pity for what could have been, had we been fully engaged.

LEADERSHIP DYNAMICS

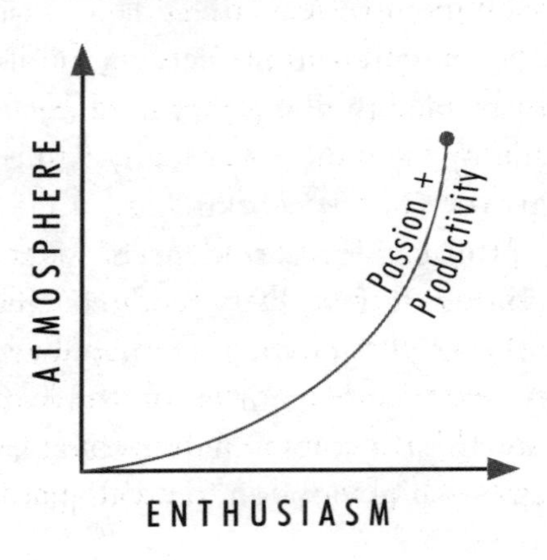

First, organizations must learn to restore passion alongside their desire for productivity. They can no longer count on productivity alone. More specifically, if they are to attract and retain talented workers and get the full value of their contribution, they must learn to respect employees' desire to be passionate about what they do. Otherwise, they risk not being able to attract sufficient qualified talent to survive. This is the essence of our entire book—to restore the soul to organizations in a way that inspires people to higher levels of contribution and achievement, or to perish as forward-thinking competitors win the battle!

Have you ever noticed that soul-inspiring workplaces consistently operate at peak levels, unlocking an "atomic explosion" of energy along with a passion for implementation? In these organizations, the rewards that come with embracing passion are unquestionable. Nor is there a debate about the value of creating passion; there is no contest between the drive for profitability and people practices. They do not typically pay better or offer extra benefits or more vacation. They do not buy passion, since it is not for sale—and cannot be bought. As such, there is no 'cost' attached to unleashing employees' passion.

Understand it is not just by implementing the ideas in this chapter that passion emerges. It cannot be easily defined through a series of how-to steps. A key ingredient is a leader's evident passion for the enormous potential of his organization. It is a feeling projected by a leader that calls forth a genuine emotional response among team members. The actions required to evoke this response cannot be described, but must be felt and transmitted to others based on the leader's commitment to this ideal. Nothing more and nothing less will do. It is about using personal persuasion to create passion.

We want to stress the crucial leadership message that people cannot be manipulated into feeling passion. The outcome of any empty effort will be a listless and cynical workforce devoid of passion, perhaps forever. While a manipulative effort may yield temporary short-term results, people will quickly see through it. When they discover the ruse (and they will), their reaction will be swift.

Instead, think of passion as a set of committed ideals put into practice—a 'special sauce' that turns the ingredients of an otherwise unremarkable meal into a taste sensation! There is no way to replace the real thing with a synthetic alternative and get the same taste.

This is why we consider enthusiasm the extra flavour dose in our 'secret recipe.' Look out when an excited bunch of enthusiastic people decide that something is going to happen! Enthusiasm is reflected in constant attention to detail, determination to achieve consistency of execution despite difficulties, and an absence of energy-draining negativity so common elsewhere. We are often stunned by the almost completely positive comments we get about these organizations, even when we solicit specific feedback about areas for improvement.

Rather than channel precious energy into complaining, people with passion channel it into doing something productive. There is a feeling of ownership that demands empowerment. They want to be part of the solution, not the problem. They willingly channel their energy into improvement efforts, because they are passionate about what they do and how they do it. Smart organizations know people's energy will be channeled somewhere, and they want to be sure it is with them! Consistent application of these practices over time breeds the passion and commitment that convert energy into positive results.

While seemingly simple, it is not that easy to practice these commitments consistently. We refer to this as a "values paradox"—easy to espouse, but hard to follow! If you do not attack this, as leader, you risk "sloganism." Once this insidious disease takes hold, it can be difficult to contain and spreads at a rapid rate. *Sloganism is the enemy of passion.* It is one of the major reasons we see for diminishing levels of passion as organizations increase in size. This can be explained by another simple equation:

SIMPLE LEADERSHIP EQUATION #6:

$$\text{Passion} = \frac{\text{Atmosphere} + \text{Enthusiasm}}{\text{Sloganism}}$$

Essentially, the passion of any organization is equal to the sum of an individual team member's enthusiasm plus the additive benefits of an organization's positive atmosphere. The presence of both is required for maximum passion. However, the presence of sloganism, even in small quantities, significantly reduces passion overall even when the other two are present. To try this, assume that each of these three factors was scaled (you may even want to think in percentage terms, for ease of interpretation) and had a value from 1 (lowest) to 100 (highest). If you chart this equation, you will find that although values can vary widely, the likely normal range for this equation is a **Passion Index** that is likely to fall between about 1 and 20 for most organizations (although the mathematical range is actually .02 to 200).

	Atmosphere (good)	Enthusiasm (good)	Sloganism (bad)	Passion Index
Company 1 (average)	60	80	20	7
Company 2 (good)	90	90	10	18
Company 3 (bad)	50	50	50	2
Absolute Maximum	100	100	1	200
Absolute Minimum	1	1	100	.02

Think about this chart for a few minutes in light of your own leadership style and organizational culture. Although we hesitate to imply that every intangible concept we are discussing can be reduced to a simple equation, we feel strongly that helping leaders to access and apply complex leadership theories can best be done by simplifying them into ready-to-use models that act as a reference point. This chart is not meant to have leaders suddenly obsess about their individual scores in each of these areas down to three decimal places, but rather to encourage leaders to actively think about how their behaviour can truly impact results. You *CAN* make a difference in people's perceptions over time, and if you focus on building a positive atmosphere while reducing sloganism at every opportunity, results in terms of increased passion will occur.

To validate this, think about most start-ups. Initially,

positive commitments exist almost by default. People want to be successful and join what they think will be a successful company. So, enthusiasm is not likely a problem. People who join companies early on are attracted to the environment of a start-up, and entrepreneurs often create organizational atmospheres that mimic their own traits. There is a common—if unspoken—set of values, and a series of challenges that help feed the team's passion. It is a time of wonder where the hours fly by and work and personal achievement are highly intertwined. However, as the organization grows, it is harder to sustain these values across a larger number of employees and customers in faraway geographies. So, an effort is usually made to articulate these values, to preserve the passion.

As this starts to happen, organizations turn to managers to ensure that 'standard' practices and policies are implemented. Often the risk for the leader is that policy begins to displace passion. Based on what we have just covered, it should be obvious this approach will fail and that it will deplete energy and enthusiasm. Instead, we recommend leaders turn to employees to seek their help in perpetuating the essence of these traits. Make employees equal partners in the quest to either become or remain passionate about what you do. Since the front lines must make it happen, they are in the best position to devise methods to make the organization successful. In turn, leadership's role is to ensure these ideals are implemented, using inclusive processes so that the cycle, even in a large workplace, can be self-sustaining and passion is the result.

This touches on the previous concepts of the nurturing role of the leader—what can you do to build a personal context for each and every employee on a daily basis that makes them feel valued and helps them sustain their passion for the purpose? Almost the entire meaning of our consulting practice can be captured in this last sentence, for we see it as the ultimate imperative of good, people-centric leadership practices. "*It's about creating passionate people!*"

The line between purposeful passion and determined passiveness is almost exclusively defined by how consistently an organization follows its heart, not just its mind. Good leaders resist sloganism and seek authenticity. They 'rule' wisely, almost like a benevolent king to his people, making sure they come first. We cannot erode our sense of commitment to our people, and doing what's fair, with the need to mitigate legal or financial risk—often the domain and primary consideration of those who make policy. Policy is an enabler of good decision-making, but is not an enabler of passion. Good leaders recognize this and ensure that their focus remains on the passion—not the policy. In the end, simply being passionate about passion itself is enough to guarantee that the rest takes care of itself!

QUESTIONS FOR REFLECTION

- How much passion do you feel about your workplace—is it an "atomic explosion" of new ideas, or has your company's idea reactor been mothballed?
- What are you passionate about, and what do you notice about what stokes your passions?
- Are you prepared to tolerate a work life that you are not passionate about? What does this imply?

DO'S AND DON'TS

- **Do** be constantly on the lookout for what the 'atmosphere' and energy of your environment are saying about people's passion levels.
- **Do** use personal persuasion to create passion and enthusiasm.
- **Do not** confuse being "at work" and "working at" something.
- **Do not** use manipulative tactics to 'make' people feel passionate; it cannot be bought.
- **Do not** allow sloganism to creep into your workplace through actions, behaviours, programs or other means.

EXERCISE FOR TEAM LEARNING

On a scale of one to ten (one is "hardly in evidence" all the way to "almost right off the scale" at ten), have each member of your team individually rate your organization's accomplishments in the areas of passion, enthusiasm and energy. In a composite score out of thirty, how does your organization score? In what areas do people agree versus disagree? What element got the highest versus lowest score? Discuss together with your leadership team (or your external coach, if you are an entrepreneur) why this might be the case. On the basis of your assessments, brainstorm an action plan you can personally and collectively implement to increase these scores as appropriate.

FIRST STEPS ALONG THE WAY

Assigned Task	*Expected Outcome*
Think about passionate versus passive behaviour. Are you sure you can identify the difference and help others be more passionate? Practice this skill frequently.	*Instills an instinct over time on how to sensitively determine others' level of passion. Making this distinction also increases your ability to act as a positive change agent in bringing more passion to the workplace.*
Examine your company's human resources practices. Are you busy trying to buy passion and loyalty, rather than building or instilling it?	*Creates recognition that passion cannot be bought, and refocuses your organization on fundamental behaviours as the basis for lasting change.*

Questions

> **To change how we talk is to change what, for our own purposes, we are.**
>
> —Richard Rorty

We were given one mouth and two ears for a reason—to spend more time listening than talking! This is *not* how we typically interact. Rather than ask, we tell. Instead of being interested in others, we are more amused by how interesting we are. Rather than listen, we prepare our responses while others talk. While listening is often recognized as a critical skill, it is sorely underdeveloped in most people's set of interpersonal abilities. Yes, we are taught in school to "*pay attention to the teacher*," but such enforced listening does not result in true hearing. If anything, the opposite ensues. Listening to the incessant chatter inside our own heads, we miss most of what happens in conversations.

This deplorable lack of attentiveness is not just individual.

Few organizations give anything but lip service to wholeheartedly listening to their workforce. Admittedly, they may hold quarterly information meetings, distribute monthly newsletters or even implement annual satisfaction surveys. Resorting to safe one-way vehicles, employees notice little discernable change from such feeble communication attempts.

How often have you been asked to answer questions on an employee survey, only to never hear anything back about the results or improvement plans? Or, if you do get feedback, for how long is the communication about action plans sustained? More often than not, we suspect your experience is like this disappointing example: on the rare occasions when employees received communications inside this company, it was about subject matter like sports scores and winning lottery tickets (not that these are bad unto themselves but we think you get our drift!), whereas initiatives like a task force to increase respect for employees petered out practically before they even started. Apparently, management was too disinterested to communicate about anything meaningful with their workforce.

And, if leaders *do* stand before employees regularly, let us hope they do not conduct their information gatherings like these two CEOs. Both were more enamoured with the sound of their own voices than with communicating simply and clearly, usually losing their audiences midway through their droning. At best, employees found their presentations a disappointing yawn. At worst, they were alienated by one leader's way of starting his meetings; to this day, we bet he has no idea how many people he turned off. Unsupportive of two-way exchanges, one CEO shut down uncomfortable questions by restating his own viewpoint, while the other's style generated virtually no questions at all.

In contrast, soul-inspiring leaders set aside personal biases to focus on others. Open to fresh ways of looking at things, they get out of their own way! Borrowing terminology from our coaching practices, these leaders listen at what is called Level 3—which is a highly sophisticated perspective. Level 3 is about discerning the many nuances that flow like currents beneath and around the actual words being used. It is about using all your senses to pick up the group's emotional state. Are people bored, interested, upset or enthused? What is the predominant feeling in the room? Level 3 listening places significant emphasis on what is not being spoken, and not just on what is being said.

As you can discern, Level 3 is far ahead of the typical ways we listen. Like our CEOs, we stay at Level 1—which is listening to what is going on inside our own heads. A self-centred way of interacting, it is about paying attention only to our own reactions to others' words and preparing our responses before the person has even finished talking. If we were honest, how often does each of us do that? If we move up to Level 2 listening, we are at least hearing more of what the other person is saying, but are still missing subtler cues and signals. At least there is some attention paid to the conversation, through words, verbal clues and body language, but we kid ourselves if we believe that is the extent of what happens in a complete dialogue.

So, how do soul-inspiring leaders manage to listen with such depth? One common trait we find is that their listening begins with a genuine interest in what the other person has to say; they make people feel special. These leaders invite them to lower defenses. With an unmistakable desire to get to know the real you, they actively seek to find out what you value, believe, need and want. Well beyond the superficial "*How's the wife and kids?*" interested leaders engage in meaningful discussions that root out core information. Realizing all of us fear rejection and hope for acceptance, they look for opportunities to make colleagues feel treasured.

Profoundly committed to making a difference in people's work lives, soul-inspiring leaders continuously ask: "*How can we do things better for you—make it a better company, live up to your expectations, or anything else you need?*" Because they have taken time to develop relationships, they are able to listen for individuals' deeper life commitments and can use that knowledge to serve others' needs. They count on team members to give them the straight goods. Standing for transformation of the workplace, they will stop at almost nothing to act on what they learn. Others feel the potent impact of their leader's dedication, enthusing them to rally their best efforts in support of the cause.

As seekers, soul-inspiring leaders ask more questions than give answers. In fact, the fewer answers you have, the better! This provocation is the antithesis of how executives are typically schooled. Called upon to make instantaneous decisions about a multitude of things in any given day, they are expected to know everything about anything. The net effect is that they begin to invent a reality where "being in charge" equates to "being in the know." What would followers think of a leader who did not have all the answers... right?

We have labeled this phenomenon the "myth of the mighty." Anybody who has worked for a leader who exhibits this trait can identify with what we are saying. Yet, executives who think of themselves as "the mighty" remain in complete denial of this phenomenon. Just like anybody else, leaders do not know everything, despite their best intentions to demonstrate otherwise!

The "myth of the mighty" has its roots in followers, too. We often expect our leaders to have more answers than questions, looking to them for guidance on how to proceed with confidence. In fact, the Western world has pretty much based its entire model of leadership on providing answers. However, while most leaders assume they need to know everything, the speed of business today makes answers more elusive than ever. Definitive answers are not easy to come by.

In our experience, true leaders understand that the best way to develop answers is to seek input and counsel from the many rather than the few. This requires letting go of the myth and not pretending you have all the answers. These pseudo-leaders are not fooling anyone, anyway. Instead, soul-inspiring leaders ask questions based on their own deep thoughtfulness and reflection, in order to bring forth others' inner wisdom.

What a different way of engaging in dialogue than asking with the so-called correct answer already in mind. Stop asking questions as the expert, and start asking without having preconceived opinions about how people should answer. It is the distinction between asking questions to obtain data and asking to unearth personal feelings or needs. The former offers authentic clues about others' state of being or motivation, while the latter yields analysis, reasons and justifications. One leads to interrogation and builds defenses, while the other removes barriers and creates powerful relationships.

Two leaders come to mind to illustrate these points. In one situation, the leader used to ask one team member without fail on Monday mornings how her weekend was, only to pass by everyone else's doorways without so much as a "*hello.*" Imagine the effect of this leader's ignorant disregard for people's feelings. We hasten to add that the minute he wanted something from those he usually ignored, his demeanour miraculously shifted. These sudden about-faces of feigned interest often made associates' heads spin, as in, "*What was that all about?*"

More damaging still was the second leader's "gotcha" questions, designed to ram her rightness down others' throats. Never asked simply to obtain facts, her questions were always spun with an intention to trap her 'victims.' Employees used to call her "The Black Widow" to denote her lethal character. Incapable of releasing her ego, the Black Widow teaches us what happens when we ask questions from a place of blame and criticism. Mired inside a vicious circle, her sphere of influence was limited to dichotomies—right/wrong, win/lose. Black or white, no gray. All or nothing and no in-between. The possibility of allowing both parties to be right literally could not be squeezed into her puny consciousness.

In case you are wondering, we are not saying that listening and asking must equate to agreeing. If you disagree, simply acknowledge others' comments. It takes far greater leadership courage to step back rather than push harder to superimpose your world on theirs. At the funeral of former Canadian prime minister Pierre Elliott Trudeau, his son recounted, in his eulogy, some valuable advice received: "*Justin, never attack the individual. We can be in total disagreement with someone without denigrating them as a consequence.*"

Respect differences by asking non-aggressive questions, summarizing what is being said, checking understanding and validating the feelings being expressed. Instead of asking "*Why?*" encourage dialogue using the many great open-ended questions at your disposal (what, where, when, who, how). Questions that start with 'why' generally promote defensiveness and closed-ended responses. Become comfortable with silence—it is a powerful conversational tool. Instead of leaping to fill dialogue gaps, allow your colleagues space and time to reflect and formulate their own well-considered responses.

Working hand in glove, listening and asking questions generate significant individual and collective benefits. Listening by seeking to understand results in being listened to. Knowing they will be given ample air time, employees no longer compete for your attention like children tugging at their teacher's skirt or pant leg. Listening without interjecting gains more information. Deep listening wins trust. At an organizational level, leaders honestly cannot afford not to listen, given how desperately workplaces need each and every employee's creativity and initiative. Examine the spiraling costs of not listening to customers and other stakeholders, evidenced in duplication of effort and costly rework—we think you will concur.

Business benefits aside, soul-inspiring leaders employ powerful listening and sincere questioning to open doors to exploration, discovery and insight. How tremendously uplifting could our exchanges be if we listened with a generosity that dignifies the individual? What extraordinary learning could be unleashed if we asked meaningful questions that promote self-actualization? All is possible when we mine team members' innate wisdom, for asking questions in this way leads to answers far richer than the leader could have brought preconceived to the exchange.

QUESTIONS FOR REFLECTION

- How interested are you, as far as approaching conversations with a genuine desire to understand people better?
- What do you notice about others' reactions to your questions in terms of body language, facial expression and other clues (are they defensive or not)?
- What factors support or detract from your listening, and what actions can you take to listen at deeper levels?

DO'S AND DON'TS

- **Do** set aside your personal biases to focus on others; move to Level 3 listening.
- **Do** focus your interactions on getting to know the 'real you' beneath the surface of those with whom you interact daily.
- **Do** summarize what is being said, check for understanding, validate feelings, ask open-ended questions and use silence.
- **Do not** confuse listening and asking with agreeing; know you can disagree without making the other person wrong.
- **Do not** hang onto the "myth of the mighty."
- **Do not** ask questions with your own correct answer already in mind.

EXERCISE FOR TEAM LEARNING

For one week, practice having no answers to team members' questions. Even if they hound you for your opinion, do not give it. You are allowed to ask questions, however. Dedicate yourself to only asking questions in all your exchanges over the next seven days. Notice the effect on people. Notice how difficult or easy it was to have no answers. Were you tempted to insert your opinion, or were you comfortable letting others have the answers? At the end of the week, bring your team together and have a dialogue about what they noticed in their interactions with you. Have them answer the same questions as you did for yourself. Talk about what you all learned and what aspects of this exercise you would like to keep as an ongoing part of your interactions.

FIRST STEPS ALONG THE WAY

Assigned Task	*Expected Outcome*
Make time for regular reflection in the workplace (e.g., organize how your business runs so everyone gets a quiet period each business day). This does not need to consume exorbitant amounts of time; regularity is more important than duration.	*Promotes introspection and validates the positive benefits of making it permissible for employees to consider important questions and create new opportunities, just by 'staring out the window'.*

Assigned Task	*Expected Outcome*
Incorporate questions into as many company communication vehicles as possible. Start with weekly team meetings, where each person reports on their objectives by answering a set of four or five key questions. Encourage them to describe what is working and what is standing as a barrier through your own thought-provoking questions as unit leader.	*What you ask as a leader is where people put their attention and action. If you ask about what is important, it will get done (this is called the "expect-inspect link"). Asking questions about how you can help others be successful conveys your genuine interest in them as people.*

Relationships

> **The key to the ninety-nine is the one... how you treat the one reveals how you regard the ninety-nine, because everyone is ultimately one.**
>
> —Stephen Covey

When we look back over our careers, we can readily come up with many examples of retirement speeches in which departing employees consistently cited the profound impact that connections developed over the years held in their recollections about corporate life. Always the theme—relationships are what really matters.

While occasionally mentioning challenging projects or assignments, they are not what had enduring value in people's memories. No. Inevitably, retirees most fondly carried with them the lingering impact of friendships begun through work, and how those relationships would sustain them in the next chapter of their lives.

When we have left organizations to move on to new adventures, saying goodbye to teammates was for us the hardest part of leaving. While often short-tenured compared to retiring veterans, we nonetheless noticed how much we had shared with our closest colleagues, without whom some of the experiences we endured would have seemed almost unbearable. Although years have now passed since our departures, we still recall the wonderful conversations with people wishing us well in our journeys.

By the way, have you ever observed that what people say about their relationships is extremely profound during these transition times of life—as if they finally feel a sense of permission to fully express what they mean to each other? We certainly wish more daily organizational conversation were this meaningful. In any case, to say that these dialogues hold a lifelong place in our hearts would be no exaggeration.

In turn, when we have each experienced the challenges of employment termination, we can speak about the power of relationships in healing traumatic hurts. If it were not for the former colleagues (besides friends and family) who reached out to offer so much support, we sometimes wonder how we would have made it through some of our darker days. Without a doubt, we count as a definite part of our success in getting back on our feet the many kindnesses offered us during those difficult times.

Perhaps as a result of our direct experiences with how much relationships contribute to professional and personal success, we have also become highly conscious about how we enter new workplaces. Just as our conduct when resigning speaks volumes about personal integrity and dignity, so does our entry into organizations. Because our ability to build solid relationships forms the foundation for all that follows, it impacts directly upon the ways others subsequently listen to and treat us. A choice point presents itself. We can either enter as bulls in a china shop, finding fault with everyone and everything, or we can glide gracefully into new environments, mindful of resident personalities.

As such, we have found that relationships seemingly doomed to a rocky start turned around so much that those same colleagues now would "*go to the moon*" for us (their words). What we did was deliberately turn around areas of disagreement by looking for commonality in our viewpoints. If you want to test this for yourself, think of two workplace relationships of your own—one positive and one challenging. Chances are, relationships make all the difference. Where there are difficulties, we find upset and an insufficient sense of relatedness. Where there are smooth-flowing relationships, we find mutual trust and respect. Before we realized the power of purposefully creating powerful relationships, we each admit—with some horror—to having missed many chances at building more positive connections with others.

To reinforce how relationships underpin everything we do, allow us to share a model that demonstrates the **building blocks to success:**

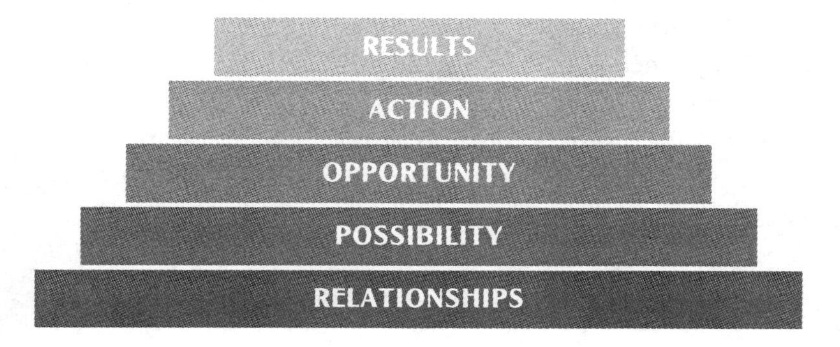

The model begins with *Relationships*; they are the bedrock on which subsequent steps are laid. Observe that we do not even consider results until there has been an explicit and full discussion that encompasses our preferred communication methods, how we will process through work and a list of many other considerations that are typically overlooked or assumed at this point. Rather than rush past relationships as a "nice to do," we make it a "must do" without which the foundation will crumble.

The next building block, *Possibility*, refers to generating and creating ideas with others, based on the possibilities we together see. We move from building strong personal rapport (through Relationships) into generating a set of "blue-sky" possibilities. "Blue sky-ing" means we think strategically and in big-picture terms to imagine what is possible through our relationship. Often, the thought of bringing possibility into the discussion does not occur to people as a planful conversational point, whereas for us it is non-negotiable.

The building block of Possibility is followed by *Opportunity*. Only now do we start moving into considering strategy and plans. We translate the opportunities we see into a more tangible direction, and craft plans to execute our strategy. Notice how much activity preceded this dialogue about opportunity.

Only when the cornerstones of Relationship, Possibility and Opportunity are firmly in place do we move into *Action* and *Results*. Notice that Action and Results follow from putting in place the other cornerstones, and not the other way around. Typical 'planning' rushes into action, while we find spending time on Relationships upfront more often than not saves considerable time in the end.

Our Relationships Model states that how we are connected links directly to results. This perspective is completely contrary to Western socialization. Taught to get down to business, we totally minimize what we term the fuzzy people-stuff in favour of getting on with the task at hand. Who needs relationships, we believe. We have so much to learn from other traditions.

In cultures where relationships are sacred, significant time is devoted first to social engagement; it is a deeply valued pillar of business success. Like it or not, Western leaders will be forced to examine their learned belief systems if they are to survive in the world of cross-cultural commerce. While it was once possible to impose a singular focus on task, our shrinking global village now insists North American leaders accede to the alternative wisdom of other cultures. In our view, this will bring about a healthy shift from task to people.

Re-balancing is what we are suggesting. Obviously, if leaders were to solely focus their line of sight on people without an eye toward results, companies would soon go out of business. This unrealistic model is no more effective than paying attention to task at the expense of people. For leaders with "hurry-up sickness," we recognize it can feel plodding to get to know people. Taking time to simply be with colleagues is seen as robbing action-oriented leaders of precious opportunities to get more work done. Task-focused, they view people investment as a huge time-waster.

Ultimately, we face a chicken-and-egg scenario. Which comes first? Should relationship-building precede goal achievement, or should it be viewed as a result of successfully completing work? An especially task-focused director we know firmly believed teamwork would magically evolve from having his team focus on a high-performance goal. At the time of one particular goal-setting exercise, relationships in Ian's team were at best mediocre. There were some strong connections, but mostly people did not understand one another's roles and responsibilities, nor did they respect him as their leader. Despite these disparities, Ian essentially ordered associates to focus on the team's goal. His idea was that, by narrowing their field of vision to concentrate on outcomes, they would achieve in the process a united spirit of camaraderie.

While we can report that the team accomplished their goal, we can also say it was strictly because their bonuses depended on it! Their sense of jubilation upon completion had nothing to do with improved team relationships, and everything to do with more money in their bank accounts! Without a doubt, they reached their target strictly as individuals, not as a cohesive unit. Interested only in doing the bare minimum to the get the job done, they created for the project manager charged with bringing them together a task about as pleasant as a root canal!

This story reinforces that it is possible to achieve results without relationships. How much more powerful could the team's accomplishments have been, however, had they engaged in team building first? If they had spent more time upfront understanding each person's needs and developing true relationships with one another, we suggest achieving results would have naturally followed. In fact, people would have likely experienced the authentic team spirit for which Ian was supposedly aiming all along.

We base our comments on the belief system that people are professionals with the personal pride to get the task done, and done well. Unlike cattle, we should not need to continuously prod them. To focus on task is for us to focus on that which should be a given in performing the job. In our world, relationship building is the means to leveraging results. It is integral to and not separate from goal attainment. Without conscious effort spent on relationship-building, we absolutely believe long-term results will inevitably suffer.

For us, soul-inspiring leadership starts with designing one's interactions according to the Relationships Model—rooted in a firm commitment to create connections that honour others. Perhaps intuitively, soul-inspiring leaders recognize the "oneness" of humanity. Realizing we are profoundly interconnected, they see themselves as one with—not separate from—their followers. Neither independent in Lone Ranger fashion, nor dependent in dysfunctional ways, they achieve results by collaborating with others. A high degree of interdependence characterizes these leaders' relationships.

While it takes some leadership courage to depend for your results on relatedness rather than on people's basic obligation to fulfill their employment contracts, we are unshakeably convinced you will see quantitative and qualitative results if you follow the "high road." Soul-inspiring leaders strive to create deep belonging, instead of treating people as mere entries in the company's human resources information system. They build relationships based on true partnership and connection, rather than mouthing "*we're one, big happy family*" platitudes while employees feel alone and forgotten in the overarching quest for results above all else. As Robin Sharma so eloquently writes: "*When we are born, we cry and others rejoice. Live your life in such a way that when you die, others cry and you rejoice.*"[3]

QUESTIONS FOR REFLECTION

- What percentage of your typical workday do you devote to tasks versus relationships, and would you change your focus in any way?
- Can you say something personal about each of your direct reports? If not, how can you make a concerted effort to develop such a relationship with each person?
- What if you considered every interaction with the people you work with to be your last? How would that perspective change the quality of your relationships?

DO'S AND DON'TS

- **Do** treat relationship building as integral to, not separate from, goal attainment.
- **Do** assume people are professionals with the personal pride to get the job done.
- **Do** use the Relationships Model (Relationships, Possibility, Opportunity, Action and Results) in how you design your working relationships.
- **Do not** emphasize getting the task done at the expense of actively building relationships with everyone on your team.
- **Do not** operate from either dependence or independence (strive for interdependence in your relationships).

EXERCISE FOR TEAM LEARNING

List everyone in your life who is important to you. You may set the criteria for what "important" means to you. Beside each of their names, note the essential elements of the relationship you share and why it is so important to you. In a third column, list the last contribution they made to you in terms of your relationship. Now, think about what you last did for them. Is the relationship in balance? Do you give as well as you get? Do you feel able to provide support for those around you, and do they experience your whole self or only a part of you? If these are not in balance, then what can you do to restore balance? Put a deadline on these activities and get on with it!

FIRST STEPS ALONG THE WAY

Assigned Task	*Expected Outcome*
Schedule one-on-one time for each of your direct reports in your calendar every week. Do not allow other meetings or tasks to overrule this set time; consider it unmovable.	*Communicates loudly and clearly that you value spending time with people—particularly when they see you not sacrificing their time to other, apparently more important tasks.*

Assigned Task	*Expected Outcome*
Set out on a campaign to get to know each of your team members' personal needs—their preferred communication styles, how they wish to be held accountable, what they need to perform optimally. Also, show an interest in what is important to them outside of work.	*Demonstrates you want to get to know the real person on the inside, not just information to get them to perform better, faster, etc. Shows you wish to work with people in ways that address their needs, not just according to your own style preferences.*
Book a block of time (a half-day or a day) quarterly to 'work' alongside your employees. This can involve shadowing them as they move through their tasks, or simply making that time the employee's to structure as they see fit.	*Shows your desire to become familiar with the potential barriers and challenges that stand in the way of job satisfaction. Provides you with valuable information about issues to address and communicates your intention to continuously improve the work environment.*

NOTES

3 Sharma, Robin. *Who Will Cry When You Die?* Toronto: Harper Collins Publishers Ltd., 1999.

Servant Leadership

> **The high destiny of the individual is to serve rather than to rule.**
>
> **—Albert Einstein**

The concept of servant leadership, originated by Robert Greenleaf, is both deceptively simple and confusingly complex. It gets at the essence of leadership and has proven itself worthy of lifetime study. To be a servant leader is to be the ultimate leader.

Finding organizations that demand leaders be servants to a vision, rather than to themselves or their agenda, opens up the possibility to attain lofty goals and work in a soul-inspiring setting. This emphasis shift in a company's leadership model creates power and authority structures that breed confidence and encourage people. But there are not many. So if the concept is proven, then why are there not more examples of this in business today?

The reason has as much to do with human nature as it does leadership practice. At our core, most of us have some element of being "pleasers." We like to be liked—a natural desire. At the same time, if we were to admit it, most of us harbour some elements of self-interest in all we do, despite our efforts to control these impulses. It is normal to ask, "*What's in it for me?*" But these traits are not necessarily in sync with the demands of servant leadership.

Let us clarify. Servant leadership is not about doing what everyone else wants you to do. In fact, servant leadership demands that you not give in to the impulse to set agendas democratically. It is not about what we want, but about what the vision demands of us. It is about finding a calling so compelling that it creates, in and of itself, the desire for one to serve and do what must be done to achieve the vision—even if that takes us outside our comfort zones.

The very term "servant leadership" can be beguiling when understood this way. It is not about a weak leader attempting to please everyone else by doing what they all expect of him or her. Such a weak model is not even remotely in keeping with servant leadership. While still highly participative, because people are encouraged to serve the vision, the actual leadership role is highly directive. It requires the leader to articulate the vision's benefits clearly and engagingly.

Let us consider another critically important element of servant leadership: it must not be egocentric or self-serving. Indeed, in many historic acts of leadership that would fit this model, it was not clear the act of leadership itself promised much reward for the one leading. This is an important aspect of Greenleaf's definition.

Consider the example of Martin Luther King—often cited as a model of strength in so many respects. In our view, his utter devotion to the cause and unceasing efforts to change the civil state of an entire race is most clearly an example of servant leadership in action. He probably had more to lose personally than to gain, yet he persevered. The enormous personal risk he undertook ultimately played out in his assassination. Martin Luther King "had a dream"—a dream so many naturally shared and who willingly followed him to a better future. There was never much debate, except among his enemies, about his right to be leader of the cause. He personified it. Nor was there concern about his credibility; his acts of leadership were pure of intent and selfless.

There are other instructive historical examples, but they would all feature similar elements. Leaders who suspend their self-interest and act with a pure heart to serve in the best interests of a cause or future vision will find people willingly adopt them as natural leaders. This is indeed a calling, and a higher form of leadership than we witness in most areas of business today.

While most examples of servant leadership are often unrelated to business, we find these concepts translate very successfully into such a setting. For example, the organization must come at vision "pure of heart," which is about ensuring its existence does not have unintended negative consequences on the environment or world health. It is about balancing profits with philanthropy. There can be many other examples, but the concept is simple—*the vision must be balanced with a sense of not being promoted in one's best interests alone*. When combined, these elements provide the basis for servant-leadership practices in an organizational setting.

The last aspect of servant leadership is that, to be successful, service must be demonstrated by all the organization's leaders. We must find ways to ensure that all those endorsed as leaders truly exhibit commitment to the cause. Leaders must understand the cause is always more important than self-interest. Wayward leaders, no matter how skilled otherwise, cannot be allowed to destroy achievement of the vision through misaligned behaviour.

In our experience, this is the single biggest risk in organizations. Allow us to share two real scenarios. In one firm, a leader concocted an elaborate scheme to get her boss fired for what were patently self-serving gains. Using others' naïve trust to betray them and curry favour with senior leaders disenchanted with the department head, her manoeuvring was only caught in a bizarre twist of events at the eleventh hour. Given the fact that she was a therapist before joining this company, we leave you to draw your own conclusions about her brand of therapy.

In another example, the magnitude of personal reputation was strikingly brought home while doing an interview with a client firm. As the conversation proceeded, we discovered that we had similar knowledge about the repugnant actions of a senior officer since installed by a questionable Board of Directors in another firm. From company to company, this President had repeated the same disgusting exploits, and he now finds it hard to overcome these labels wherever he goes. Talk about the extreme opposite of servant leadership!

Yet, for whatever reason, companies tolerate behaviour from those in leadership roles contrary to their best interests. We believe this is why everyone breathes such a huge sigh of relief when senior management boldly declares that actions incongruent with stated values will not be tolerated; it is such a rarity. Terminating those individuals' employment sends unequivocal signals, whereas condoning unacceptable practices destroys hearts, shatters morale, and leaves people hopeless. If you conducted an unofficial survey to name the *"top five people who have to go,"* we believe you would have virtually one-hundred percent agreement across your organization. Everyone knows who these individuals are—it is simply a matter of having the will to do what needs to be done. This in turn sends a message to followers about the workplace's overall integrity and the desire of every leader to demonstrate the values of servant leadership.

If we reflect again briefly on the historical examples, we often note they were solitary leaders of causes who rarely had much of an organization behind them. They did not put in place charts and boxes outlining roles for managers and leaders. Instead, natural leaders simply rose to the occasion from inside the ranks of followers. In essence, supplementary leaders were almost *anointed* by other followers as examples to emulate. This is not often the case in business, though we suggest it should be.

The most fundamental principle we believe should be followed in appointing leaders is that they have earned the right to lead by demonstrating credibility with those they will be expected to lead. People desperately want to believe and trust in their leaders. They admire and seek out the qualities of integrity and trust.

Too often, though, organizations promote or hire leaders singularly for their skills. This is a mistake, evidenced by one company with which we worked. A highly capable leader (in terms of background, experience and skills) was hired to replace the resigning leader of one of the company's main divisions. While Mike unquestionably possessed specific expertise that benefited the business and some direct reports, he also had significant skill and behavioural gaps in precisely this area of servant leadership. Yes, Mike believed strongly in serving the organization's senior leadership (less than a handful of individuals); of that, there was no doubt. But when it came time to display an equal and willing attitude of service toward the rest of his extended team (some ten to fifteen individuals), Mike frankly fell short. For this most sizable portion of the firm's internal population, their primary experience was his disdain, both with them as people and as employees. His disregard was palpable, and so he also received a level of performance commensurate with his poor opinion of these support team members. For him, they were dispensable, and Mike often remarked that he wished he could just get rid of all of them and start afresh. The only 'servants' in his mind were these employees, tolerated only for how they could serve him. To remotely suggest that his role was to serve these people (and not the other way around) would have been incredulous to him.

This story illustrates the key point that a leader can possess all the greatest skills in the world, but if not accompanied by the 'right' attitude, this individual can wreak tremendous havoc within the organization. While skills are important, they are not the be-all and end-all. Rather, we assert that if you first find leaders with the right attitude, skills can be acquired and taught. Better yet, find a leader who has both. If you must choose, emphasize attitude and your organization will be unstoppable.

Whatever you do, if you want to achieve servant leadership, never tolerate behaviour that violates the best interests of the common good and the vision. To do otherwise, no matter how compelling the rationale, is to travel the slippery slope toward erosion of any true leadership promise and potential.

Finally, allow us to leave you with the gist of an e-mail forwarded to us. It speaks of the attitude of interest that is sometimes conveyed while recruiting employees and that rapidly dissipates once those same individuals are brought on board.

Food for thought... the story of a human resources director who was hit by a bus and died. Her soul was met at the Pearly Gates by St. Peter, who wound up offering her a day in Hell and a day in Heaven, and then she could choose the one in which she wanted to spend an eternity. In stepping off the elevator into Hell, she found herself on the putting green of a beautiful golf course. She played an excellent round of golf with former executive colleagues, enjoyed an excellent steak-and-lobster dinner and danced with the Devil. She returned from her twenty-four hours in Hell to lounging around on the clouds, playing the harp and singing in Heaven. In response to St. Peter's question on the heels of her twenty-four hours in Heaven and Hell, she unbelievably replied that she had a better time in Hell. So, St. Peter escorted her to the elevator and again she went back to Hell. When the doors opened, she found herself standing in a desolate wasteland covered in garbage and filth. She saw her friends were dressed in rags, picking up the garbage and putting it into sacks. The Devil came up to her and put his arm around her. "*I don't understand,*" stammered the human resources director. "*Yesterday I was here and there was a golf course and country club and we ate lobster, danced and had a great time. Now all there is are wastelands and garbage and all my friends are miserable.*" The Devil looked at her and smiled. "*Yesterday we were recruiting you. Today,* you're staff...."

QUESTIONS FOR REFLECTION

- Think about your ideal historical leadership figure, and about a leader whom you admire in your business or professional life. What most stands out about these people that makes these choices so easy?
- Are you generally a "pleaser" or not, and how does your style impact on your personal ability to lead others?
- What does serving others mean to you, and how does thinking of yourself as a servant leader sit with you?

DO'S AND DON'TS

- **Do** make sure an attitude of service is demonstrated by all the organization's leaders.
- **Do** earn the right to lead by demonstrating integrity and honouring your commitments.
- **Do** choose attitude over skill, if you must choose between two leaders to hire or promote.
- **Do not** falsely conclude a servant leader is a people "pleaser."
- **Do not** tolerate actions incongruent with stated values.

- **Do not** put your self-interest ahead of acting with a pure heart to serve the best interests of a cause or vision.

EXERCISE FOR TEAM LEARNING

Consider the most important goal that you and your team must accomplish within the next twelve months. Be very specific about its measurable outcome—how will it make a difference for your organization. Once you have this in mind, fill a single sheet of paper with specific ideas and actions that you can take as a leader to demonstrate servant leadership on this project. What could be noticeably different in your style that would have people be very certain you value getting to the outcome successfully more than you do any particular role or profile for yourself? How could you communicate daily your efforts to make the team successful by taking a supporting rather than leading role on this one? Finally, take these notes and share them with your team and ask them to demonstrate their own personal leadership by keeping you accountable for your commitments. This exercise, while challenging, will secure the project's success.

FIRST STEPS ALONG THE WAY

Assigned Task	Expected Outcome
Think about the leader to whom you currently report. Does this person exhibit the traits of servant leadership? Why or why not? If you were in his or her role, what w	*Examining leadership practices in a practical context, and applying the theories of servant leadership to these contexts, is an effective way of learning to make the concrete.*
Br to th bc de va	*otion, propels start thinking out their own leadership. By ut their money s, the provoca- to action.*
Co eit yo th he mı thi	*itical question servant leader- ization is not ractice of true r be possible.*

gy

> **Alienation, if such an overused word still has meaning, is not only the result of social systems... but of the very nature of technology: the new means of communication accentuate and strengthen non-communication.**
>
> —Octavio Paz

d economic
called the
tions point
v technolo-
argely con-
rough the
new Digital Economy. Much of this information revolution will benefit mankind in so many ways: medical advances, improved conveniences, automated services. Like all revolutions, there is also a dark side: technology as a means of increased social alienation and destruction of the human soul.

Please do not infer we are against the progress technology represents. We are not. We embrace it as a means of freeing humans from the drudgery of routine tasks easily automated. It would be foolish for anyone to reject technology or to resist learning how to master it. To ignore it is to place oneself at the margins of our technocratic society.

Instead, we want to address how to derive technology's benefits while limiting its negative implications. First and foremost when approaching critical technology decisions, soul-inspiring leaders put people ahead of technology by recognizing humans have natural limitations in adapting to advanced technologies. In their effort to preserve the emphasis on people and soul-inspiring work, they defer to the human side of the equation rather than tip the balance always in favour of deriving more cost-saving benefits from technology. In fact, what is often referred to as the "productivity paradox" (increasing investments in IT for declining improvements in productivity) may be entirely based on this typical approach to making IT investments without actually considering the people and process issues.

Interestingly, for leaders who do get this, the result is often productivity and profit levels that meet or exceed those of competitors who emphasize technology over people. The same trend can be seen in businesses that invest in improved soft skills rather than more automation. They can often attract a premium from customers who prefer and benefit from an improved "people touch," rather than an efficient "computer touch."

All this has led us to develop a theory about the implications for technology and people practices inside the modern organization that we think powerfully conveys these points. We use it in our client work to explain what we consider the two most important contributors to overall productivity levels:

SIMPLE LEADERSHIP EQUATION #7:

Productivity Threshold (%) = (Process Efficiency Factor)^2 x (People Effectiveness Factor)^2

Our equation assumes the maximum productivity of any organization is one hundred percent, but it sets a very high standard to achieve this. It would require you be one-hundred percent efficient in your business processes (measured as a factor between 0 and 1) and equally effective in your people practices (also a factor between 0 and 1). We believe this equation represents the reality organizations face today: productivity is truly a function of your ability to integrate great technology and process with winning people practices. Advances in only one side of the equation will never yield the same level of productivity as a skillful balance between the two.

To help illustrate, let us look at a table that shows representative calculated scores for an organization's productivity threshold based on quite probable values for the other two factors:

Process Efficiency	Formula Input	People Effectiveness	Formula Input	Productivity Threshold
100%	$(1)^2 = 1$	100%	$(1)^2 = 1$	(1 x 1) = 100%
99%	$(.99)^2 = .98$	99%	$(.99)^2 = .98$	(.98 x .98) = 96%
90%	$(.90)^2 = .81$	90%	$(.90)^2 = .81$	(.81 x .81) = 66%
95%	$(.95)^2 = .90$	80%	$(.80)^2 = .64$	(.90 x .64) = 58%
99%	$(.99)^2 = .98$	50%	$(.50)^2 = .25$	(.98 x .25) = 25%
50%	$(.50)^2 = .25$	50%	$(.50)^2 = .25$	(.25 x .25) = 6%

The equation may at first strike you as unbelievable. How can simply operating at less-than-perfect levels have such a devastating impact on your organization's productivity? Yet, even a very slight one percent reduction in process efficiency and a similar reduction in people effectiveness instantly yields an overall four percent reduction in productivity. We assert this is true because systemic inefficiencies or ineffectiveness impact your workplace many times over. As a soul-inspiring leader, you cannot afford to ignore the big impact small issues can have.

An example of these implications comes from our experiences with a financial service organization that has since grown to become one of Canada's largest. While its technology and processes resulted in numerous customer service improvements and institutional efficiencies, it was not achieving competitors' productivity levels. Senior management resorted to what it thought was the right course of action by deciding to improve front-line employee accountability for productivity. Yet, after two years of effort, the needle had barely moved and nothing had really changed.

Let us tell you the other side of this story—the one we hope will unlock the secret of this equation for you. If you were a teller or supervisor, you were expected to work speedily, ensuring bank lines remained short and moved quickly. You were expected to make instantaneous decisions, enforce policy and procedures, and ensure protection from fraud and loss. You were trusted with open access to hundreds of thousands of dollars, and could electronically control the movement of millions of dollars in any given shift. But you *could not make a simple mistake*.

In the company's view, all this new technology was supposed to enable perfect work. As a teller, you were expected to balance to the penny. If you had a difference, you were forced to remain after your shift at your own expense to help find it. Worse still, the technology that was so advanced in performing routine transactions provided virtually no help with simple diagnostics so you could find your mistake more quickly. These functions were "too expensive" to build into the requirements. Since they only benefited tellers, in the company's view, no investment was approved to include them.

Ironically, the same technology had been built to automatically analyze a teller's supposed performance. It could easily track average time to complete common transaction types, but did not know Jane had twenty-five frail old ladies as customers that day or how well the service had been delivered. Supervisors were supposed to know this information, but all too often relied on 'statistics.' This tended to replace an active and vital performance dialogue, disabling the relationship between employees and management. This firm broke all our cardinal rules—and was suffering the alienation of technology gone awry as a result of focusing singularly on company benefits.

While senior management felt this approach to policy improved accountability and productivity, for front-line employees it was simply unfair. One executive was so bold as to suggest that "*employees respect what management inspects*"! Yet, he seemed astonished to learn his own employees did not respect him because of his poor treatment of supposedly "*valued associates*" (a phrase taken from their two-inch thick policies and procedures manual).

So what do you think tellers did? They slowed down. They disconnected and disengaged from anything other than the desire to be seen as perfect. They learned to double-check even routine transactions, especially if they had somewhere important to go after work that day! And the lines? "*Not my problem*," they reflected to themselves. "*Customers will simply have to wait a little longer*." And the productivity threshold kicks in... they "hit the wall." There were no additional gains from investing in technology or process that would be reflected in improved productivity, because they did not get the people side of the equation right.

To begin to do something about this, first ensure that technology decisions meet the test for benefits to employees and the company. Soul-inspiring leaders always ensure technology is humanizing rather than dehumanizing. Second, always consider the rationale for any technology investments—have similar investments been made in your people practices to ensure a balanced outcome in terms of productivity? Finally, do not let technology interfere with direct and personal communication. Use it to supplement and improve these vital exchanges with employees. Find out what is really going on, in person, and then use technology to improve your speed of response to your team's issues. Watch the difference.

Technology and people practices must move in tandem to achieve maximum productivity. Use the equation and win. Get both sides of the equation right, and productivity will soar!

QUESTIONS FOR REFLECTION

- When you have had a bad technology experience, what made it that way, as contrasted with factors that contributed to a positive technology experience?
- Does your organization emphasize technology/process or people, or a balance of both?

- When have you fallen into technology/people practices traps, as did the senior manager in our story, and how can you avoid them in future?

DO'S AND DON'TS

- **Do** look for the benefit to employees and customers of any new technology before looking for a financial benefit to the organization.
- **Do** apply the productivity threshold as a constant barometer of the health of your people and process practices.
- **Do** retain your "people touch" even as you improve the efficiency of your "computer touch."
- **Do not** use technology to replace dialogue and personal communication.
- **Do not** use technology as a means to control, diminish, or eliminate people.

EXERCISE FOR TEAM LEARNING

Using our equation, calculate your organization's "productivity threshold." First, develop your own assessment of the major factors that should go into determining process efficiency and people effectiveness ratings for your organization. Then, measure and rate current performance and set targets for improvement. Bring this thinking to your next leadership team meeting and review it with your peers. Together with your colleagues, find three ways within thirty days to impact your organization's productivity threshold by improving both sides of the equation.

FIRST STEPS ALONG THE WAY

Assigned Task	Expected Outcome
Assess how you could introduce a management training course on our equation that would be of value to your organization.	*Awareness is the first step to improvement. Helping others within your organization understand the power of working both sides of the equation can have a lasting organizational impact.*
Establish a measurement system for People Effectiveness. Simple measures may include satisfaction surveys, turnover and employee referral rates, training investments in soft skills, etc. Use whatever measures are right for you.	*Often in our experience, there is lots of emphasis on measuring process and technology efficiency but not an equal amount is spent on people effectiveness. Establishing a more equitable measurement system helps correct this imbalance.*
Review your organization's leadership practices. Given the story in this chapter, are you doing any similar things to your employees? Identify and eliminate them immediately, along with an apology and a promise to ensure they will not be reinstated in future.	*Quick, decisive action to treat employees with respect and dignity always has an immediately positive impact that says you are serious about changing "the way things are around here." When sustained and implemented in conjunction with other parts of this book, you are well on your way to being a soul-inspiring leader.*

Upheaval

> The art of progress is to preserve order amid change and to preserve change amid order.
>
> —Alfred North Whitehead

Business today is essentially an Indy 500 race. Welcome to the Third Age—a state of accelerated development brought on by the arrival of the Information Age—an age that will only continue to cause social upheaval that those on the leading edge embrace rather than dispute. "We must *learn to deal with continuous upheaval*" is a mantra everyone has heard, but whose consequences not everyone has internalized.

What we do know about our wired world is this: basic leadership skills are more important than ever, even if they, too, are in a state of upheaval. Much of what we learned at some distant point no longer applies. Yet, no matter how quickly decisions must be made and implemented, leaders still need to achieve their goals with numbers of very smart people on board and behind them. There is no way to trick people on this point even if we *are* all moving more quickly than ever.

By way of example, this story, from the early part of our careers, takes place within the travel industry. While fun, it was not what we would have called the most dynamic or complex business in the world. However, in the mid-'80s, something remarkable happened—the arrival of computers on the desktops of travel agents, called "Computer Reservation Systems" (CRS). These computers, offered by the airlines to their agents for a fee, allowed them to search for and directly book flights on-line, instantly—to calculate fares and options automatically, rather than manually using old tools such as fare ladders, fare rules and official airline guides. The world was changing... and on the surface, for the better.

However, the industry was also one which attracted a certain type of person; it was often said that the *"business got into your blood."* You either loved it or hated it. And, those that stayed were usually committed to it as a career choice. One such lady was Kathleen, a lovely Scottish woman of a certain age who had been in the business for years. In fact, she had probably been in the business for more years than we had yet walked the Earth during this story.

Working in the field, we were involved in the design, development and installation of these systems to improve travel agency productivity. These systems were state-of-the-art at the time and offered individual agents and their employers incredible advantages. They were easy to use, saved time, increased profits and made an agent's work easier to accomplish. Who would not want to use a CRS to make airline bookings?

Well… Kathleen did not. For all the supposed good this "thing" on her desk was going to do for her, we had not yet realized there was another perspective on this "advance in the industry." We were blind to the fact that this technology represented a new and scary skill that was not easy for everyone to acquire. That it made Kathleen feel like her life's work was worth nothing, because everything she knew was no longer valuable or necessary. That the industry was going to become dominated by "*those young-un's who learned this stuff when they were kids,*" and that her knowledge would fall by the wayside in the move to automate her world. As far as she was concerned, this significant upheaval was going to leave her behind and out in a cold and unforgiving world that no longer wanted her. So, what do you think she did?

Well, she valiantly tried to resist change at every turn. And we got angry and frustrated. Our project, in this rather large office of a major travel chain, was going well with everyone except Kathleen. And our contract probably depended on this first one going well. Yet no amount of fact about how much better her job would be seemed to entice her onto the learning curve required to master using a computer. What were we going to do?

We ended up causing her to leave, perhaps before they fired her. Young, smart and technically savvy (if naïve), we quickly saw an opportunity to inform the director of operations of the chain about the fact that the manager of this location was obviously not "*dealing with the tough people issues.*" Kathleen not only left this particular agency, she left a business she loved altogether and went to work for some faceless, nameless corporation north of the city. We saw it as a victory for progress. We do not know how she saw it.

Looking back on this story of twenty years ago, we recognize, as many of you do, just how pathetic a response this was to a very understandable situation. Yet at the time, the upheaval in Kathleen's life was actually only progress in ours. This juxtaposition meant there was no way to reconcile our feelings toward each other, because they were set up as a conflict.

Many years later, we sought out Kathleen (at some effort to locate her, we should point out), to apologize for what we had done. By this time, she had long since forgotten (forgiven?) what had happened and was happy doing what she was doing. However, we felt the need to get closure with Kathleen, because she was the victim of our uncaring as souls and leaders. In retrospect, and with what we know now, we would have approached the situation very differently. Nothing would have changed about the imperative to adopt technology, the demand for increased productivity and speed, and our need as leaders in the business to ensure all of this happened. What would have changed is our approach.

We would have smothered Kathleen in the knowledge of how valuable her wisdom about the business was. We would have reassured her that while the computer was going to change what she did, it was not going to change how she did it. Her clients would still benefit from her gentle and patient ways. She would make the transition, over time, and be part of our extraordinary team.

We would have sent her out well ahead of time to get basic computer literacy training, at the company's expense and during work time, and encouraged her by buying her a card that said "*way to go*" every time she attempted to learn a new skill by completing a course. We would have appointed her our "process coach" on the project and given her the task of ensuring that, while we automated the mundane work of making airline bookings, technology did not become a substitute for the "personal touch" for which she was so famous.

We would have encouraged her to work with all the staff, to help them balance "high tech with high touch." We would have ensured she understood that, while we cannot avoid upheaval, we did not equate this with any loss in her personal value to the business. In fact, as we automated, there was more than ever a need for the attitudes and motives of such an experienced employee to be encouraged in others.

Kathleen was her usual gentle self in our meeting, and made us feel very much like we had nothing to apologize for. But we did. We had wounded her soul. Not with intent, but still with impact. That is what 'unconscious' leaders do. In the name of progress, they wound.

To be clear—we are not judging those among you who may resonate with this story, for this lesson cannot often be avoided until it happens to you. And it will. So, when will you will be a Kathleen? Does this have to happen to you before you recognize that there are so many more productive ways to deal with systemic upheaval?

During such times, leaders must constantly balance sets of apparently competing scales: the need to be "in control" while staying receptive, the impetus to be quick to decide and yet reflective. Like a true paradox, both sides demand equal attention by causing a constant push-pull between these polarized priorities. To circle back to where we started, that is why no one specific leadership style can any longer be uniformly effective. Instead, what is required is the ability to constantly apply the most appropriate leadership style to a rapidly changing set of situations faced by your workplace.

If your organization is moving in "web time," so too will any problems you face! No matter how great the stress engendered by the "need for speed," leaders must still take responsibility for slowing down long enough to look around them at the varying reactions to upheaval. They must respond to each individual's needs, one person at a time. We think of this as a "slow down" approach that will ultimately allow you to go fast. Remember, what works for Kathleen does not necessarily apply to other members of your team, and vice versa!

QUESTIONS FOR REFLECTION

- When in your life have you wounded someone's soul in the name of progress, even if it was not intentional? Are there repairs to be made?
- What is one immediate action you will take with a 'resistant' team member, based on the positive learning you gleaned from the story about Kathleen?
- How can you harness the wisdom of longer-tenured employees to help you avoid the pitfalls of poor execution of the "need for speed"?

DO'S AND DON'TS

- Do practice seeing upheaval from all the perspectives you can think of.

- **Do** help others around you who are struggling with upheaval to reshape their (negative) thoughts into a more positive framework, using approaches that work for them.
- **Do not** assume that upheaval means you leave behind good basic leadership skills.
- **Do not** expect everyone on your team to have the same reaction as you do to "advances in the industry."
- **Do not** think any amount of fact is going to necessarily help someone who is struggling with upheaval to embrace it.

EXERCISE FOR TEAM LEARNING

Ask everyone on your team the question, "*If you were to lose your job tomorrow, what would you do and why?*" Help them to view this situation as an opportunity rather than a threat by encouraging planning (financially, personally and professionally) for this 'event' in their careers. Help them 'expect' it at some inevitable point in the future. Assisting others to have the resources they need to be self-sufficient for a period of time will give them a greater freedom to embrace this kind of upheaval rather than fear it. Have everyone write out their "plan to progress to freedom," and encourage them to track their progress. Reminding them to keep this plan current ensures you all maintain the freedom from fearing job change.

FIRST STEPS ALONG THE WAY

Assigned Task	*Expected Outcome*
Identify one aspect of a current work process or activity that you could improve. Write down in no more than three sentences the rationale for this change and why it should be made. Communicate it to others and see how they respond.	*Helps you begin to realize that no matter how justified a change may be, it can still be threatening. Provides learning around adapting the "need for change" with the "speed of change," and shows how to get people onside through appropriate leadership rather than justification of your actions.*
Think about your current professional context. What is the next big upheaval you expect and how can you plan to harness its power to create positive outcomes?	*Restores your appreciation for competitive and contextual scanning, and contributes to learning how to embrace upheaval as a positive force.*
Talk with your parents, siblings or others in your family about upheaval. What allowed you to change, or not, various aspects of your relationships within your family in response to changes in circumstances, life events, etc.?	*Draws out patterns you have perhaps learned about how to cope with upheaval from your family dynamics. Can you assess them dispassionately, and either keep or reject your feelings about upheaval based on this examination?*

Values

> What you are shouts so loudly in my ears I cannot hear what you say.
>
> —Emerson

Nobody reading this book would fail to recognize the hallmark of soulless workplaces—the beautifully crafted wall plaque prominently displayed, but nowhere evidenced in people's daily work lives. We all recognize them—documents wordsmithed at exorbitant cost by consultants working with senior leaders in spare-no-expense retreat settings. We have all watched the leadership team file back into the workplace, "Sermon from the Mount" ready to proclaim to the "unwashed masses" the wisdom of their magnificent effort. Jaded, we predict what the scrolls will say—"*People are our greatest asset*," "*We create shareholder value through our dedicated team of employees*," "*Customers are number one*"—or very close approximations. We all know the impact on employees during special communication sessions. Wondering what their leaders were smoking, they are left with the puzzled sense we must be describing someone else's company, for the values in no way resemble their own! Are we right? You bet we are.

Why such dissonance? In our view, it is not necessarily large-scale corruption that characterizes valueless organizations (although the press is rife with these stories at the time of writing). Rather, it is the insidious effect of accumulated 'little' unsavory actions that debase people and eat away their souls—politicking, playing favourites, manipulating, jockeying for position. A former colleague likens the phenomenon to a *"dead fish on a table in the middle of the living room."* Everyone sees its decaying ugliness and smells its stench, but no one is gutsy enough to declare the truth. It is appalling how often this goes on, yet everyone colludes in turning a blind eye.

For instance, how people are exited from an organization provides the perfect vehicle for practicing alignment between one's stated values and actual actions. Based on direct personal experience, we can attest that the degree of sensitivity and dignity applied to this emotionally-charged event speaks volumes. Unfortunately, we find employers more often miss the mark than not by hurrying people unceremoniously out the door. What a missed opportunity to offer compassion to the shocked individual! What a failure to calm traumatized employees left in these departing individuals' wake, for survivors often become the silent wounded, more so than the person who eventually moves on with his or her life.

What a difference it would have made to gather people several times in one day in the company boardroom—both immediately at the time of the announcement and then again near the close of business, with small group and individual check-ins interspersed between. What an opportunity it would have provided to create closure, by allowing exiting employees to stay long enough to say goodbye if they chose. In a company that is very unused to layoffs, these equally true positive actions went far toward helping people heal their shock and grief.

In fact, let us spend some time considering how layoffs, downsizing, plant closings and restructuring are handled. Under pressure, the veneer quickly peels. Are frontline workers first to have their employment terminated while executives retain their full compensation? Or, do top brass first cut their pay during tough times? What about status barriers that underlie value discrepancies? As long as reserved parking places and other titular perks separate the "haves" from the "have-nots" we cannot in all honesty think of workplaces as values-centric. "*But I earned these rights by clawing my way to the top. I've put in my time and I deserve it,*" you might protest, to defend these contentious policies. From employees' vantage point, how would you perceive applying time clocks only to some individuals, while others are free to come and go as they please? These are vital questions, given groundswell calls for character in business life.

At this time, the possibility of spiritual values dominating business would seem far away. Evidence the proliferation of war references at work—*jungle*, *battlefield*, *enemies*—and you will perceive little room for so-called soft values. In contrast, examine the values of one workplace—*fairness*, *harmony* and *cooperation*, *courtesy* and *humility*, *gratitude*. While all may not apply in every setting, we find underlying relevance in doing something bigger than oneself, treating others with respect, being selfless through teamwork and expressing appreciation.

To share an example, one of our mutual workplaces in many ways successfully blended so-called hard and soft values. Crafted in painstaking detail by the founding partners, this organization operates by what it calls The Big Six Values—three 'hard' and three 'soft.' While apparently conflicting, they actually complement one another perfectly. For instance, one can achieve solo High Performance, but if at the expense of Teamwork, results are compromised. While Customer Accountability is strongly emphasized, if there is no Continuous Learning from customers' feedback, creative solutions get lost. One might have great Strategic Entrepreneurship, but if imposed without Open-Mindedness toward others' inventiveness, what started as a benefit is apt to fall on deaf ears.

SIMPLE LEADERSHIP EQUATION #8:

Accomplishment = *What* x *How*
(results) (values congruence)

Here again, a Simple Leadership Equation helps us articulate the way in which two factors (results and values) working in tandem lead to accomplishment. As previously, we measure both aspects of this equation in terms of a percentage from 0 to 100 percent. Quickly one can see that results alone will not cut it—true *accomplishment* lies in getting the full result while remaining values congruent. In our experience, many organizations tend to overemphasize results while underestimating the importance of adhering to values. This creates a "results at any cost" culture that ultimately depletes long-term performance and diminishes true accomplishment.

Everyone's challenge in the company example we noted above was to continuously balance competing values. This is why individual performance was evaluated according to what people accomplished (results) plus how they achieved results (values congruence). Both must be constantly juggled. To achieve dynamite results at the expense of any value is as unacceptable as adhering to soft aspects while never performing up to standard, delighting customers or thinking like a business owner. This highlights the critical need to align human resources systems to completely support stated values—systems such as recruiting, selecting and hiring, structuring, learning and developing, performance management, rewarding, communicating and decision making.

What helped team members live according to a common understanding of The Big Six were well-communicated definitions with behavioural statements describing exactly what they should say or do to demonstrate the value. The values were constantly 'refreshed' by cross-functional employee task forces who sought input from everywhere in the organization. Regular communication about progress was seen as pivotal to creating true engagement. As a result, associates' warm response to their colleagues' work was absolutely the polar opposite of the cold hearts and vacant stares that typically greet leadership visioning done in isolation.

This organization's methods are also totally unlike a cut-and-paste job we became aware of while on a coaching assignment. In this case, the company's owner borrowed a respected firm's credo by changing a word here and there. Talk about dishonest! We can only suppose what messages this President directly and indirectly communicated. At minimum, employees must have wondered if they were not unique enough to merit their own guiding values! Even worse in some ways than inheriting a set of values without involvement from one's own leaders, this story points to an unethical grasp of what it means to craft unassailable guiding principles.

Conversely, the Big Six example illustrates its founders' single-minded focus as "chief values stewards." Both through their original creation and their continuous revitalization, the CEO and senior leadership team personally took great pride in the values, making sure their support was visible and consistent. Such leadership commitment to practice what one preaches keeps hope alive. Trust and respect are essential ingredients in accepting leaders' vision; there must be unquestioned alignment between the talk and walk. The talk must be about promoting and reinforcing what the organization stands for at each and every opportunity, while the walk is evidenced in action.

Without values, people feel like hypocrites, as their personal integrity slowly slips into oblivion. Increasingly, they will no longer tolerate being associated with dishonest organizations, opting instead to work in settings aligned with their personal values. Due to the ever-changing employment landscape, workplaces will soon have no choice but to heed workers' hue and cry for this congruence between personal and organizational values.

In our profession, much ado is made of the "new contract." It is typically expressed from the employer's viewpoint as a sneering disregard for employees' ability to choose where they work—a contemptuous "*better get on the bandwagon and do as we say, not as we do.*" What gets overlooked is the demographic reality that there are no longer ten employees in line behind each person who leaves in disgusted resignation. This factor alone will force employers to adapt to the new contract as it is actually unfolding, and not with the deluded belief "*we can always get more where they came from.*"

In the new world, people will vote with their feet, leaving the valueless 'dinosaurs' for workplaces where their souls' cries are answered through character-based leadership, impeccable morals and complete values alignment. During these times of tumult and transformation, unswerving organizational values act as forces for stability. Like a sanity check, they become the one unbending benchmark to which battered employees can turn when all else is constantly shifting. Values anchor people. They stand as bulwarks when unrelenting external pressures make work life feel like quicksand beneath one's feet. Values are the last bastion, and continuously changing priorities must never be permitted to displace the organization's fundamental commitments.

QUESTIONS FOR REFLECTION

- What do you notice about the degree of alignment between your values and those professed by your organization, and do any actions suggest themselves?
- To what degree would you be prepared to compromise your values until you had reached a point beyond which it would be personally intolerable?
- How can businesses guard their values in the cold, hard, real world?

DO'S AND DON'TS

- **Do** treat people in dignified and values-based ways during layoffs, downsizings, closings, restructuring and termination.
- **Do** align your human resources systems to completely support stated values (e.g., recruiting, selecting and hiring, structuring, learning and developing, performance management, rewarding, communicating, decision-making).
- **Do** think of yourself as a "chief values steward," who consistently practices what you preach.
- **Do not** fall into deluded belief systems about the "new employment contract" as meaning people will continue indefinitely to work for valueless 'dinosaur' organizations.
- **Do not** evaluate performance solely according to what people accomplish at the expense of how they achieve results (i.e., values).

EXERCISE FOR TEAM LEARNING

Do an informal survey among a cross-section of your employee population (e.g., direct reports, functional and leadership peers, making sure to include new hires) to determine what percentage can not only recite your values, but can also translate specifically what they mean to them personally. What did you observe? If there are gaps, go back to the people you polled to ask about actions needed to address the dissonance. Ask for their help in implementing these actions.

FIRST STEPS ALONG THE WAY

Assigned Task	Expected Outcome
To develop a crisp set of statements outlining both what you and your company stand for, brainstorm three to five major values in two themes—personal and business. Hone these two sets of statements so you have up to five sentences of less than ten words each in both categories.	*By taking every opportunity to communicate what you stand for personally, employees get to know you as a human being, not just as a figurehead. Having a prepared set of succinct statements describing the company's values educates people who may be unfamiliar with this information and creates engagement.*
Begin your next meeting with the question: "*What kind of company do you want to work for?*" Take careful notes.	*Gets employees to start thinking about what they value. Provides a springboard for a return visit to share what you believe in—tied to individuals' comments—so you can ultimately create a vision everyone believes in.*
Assign all your employees to create their own personal mission statements. Determine the means by which these statements will be shared within and across teams. Conduct semi-annual checkups to verify if alignment continues to exist between personal and organizational visions.	*Helps team members see how their personal mission connects with the organization's mission and how they can make both come alive. Also surfaces areas of misalignment, so individuals can be helped to make the right choices (either inside the company or by moving to another organization).*

Wealth

> **We make a living by what we get, but we make a life by what we give.**
>
> —Winston Churchill

For as long as economists have examined wealth, it has been concentrated in the hands of a few. The fortunate, or in some cases ruthless, few mostly built wealth by accumulating valuable assets and deploying them to secure self-sustaining income streams. Examples include fortunes created in the railroad, oil, mining, and automobile industries, to name a few. With corporate success has come an assumption about material wealth: our society often views the extent of one's ability to accumulate material goods as testaments to success. This has caused deep divides, especially among those toiling for low wages, since exploitation of cheap labour has been and continues to be used to create incredible wealth for the few.

We have a different view of emerging future wealth. The

new wealth will not be created from industrial infrastructure, but from knowledge and creativity. Therefore, the potential for new wealth is locked up in the hearts and minds—the very souls—of people. As a result, the focus of any successful business must shift from wealth accumulation (a physical assets model) to wealth creation (a knowledge management model). We believe this bold statement holds up under scrutiny and will emerge as a major revision to the entire realm of future economic thinking.

What would support such a position? One needs to look no farther than the "dot.com" revolution to see this concept unfolding in practice. While we acknowledge the market's intense ardor for Internet company stocks has cooled to more rational levels, that is not the point. Rather, consider the underlying principles of how these businesses have created, and will create, whatever wealth the markets ascribe to them. Most have virtually no physical assets. In fact, the phrase "*our assets walk out the door every night to go home*" takes on new meaning in most high-tech businesses today. Even if they do have physical assets, their stated intent is to minimize investment in "bricks" and deploy it primarily to support on-line, "clicks" business models.

And what about actually transacting business? What are most Internet businesses if not the definition of "virtual"? They are simply a collection of millions of lines of code, developed by very smart people, running on computers that could be anywhere, accessed by customers over networks from their homes, businesses or even portable phones. This defines the essence of our theory: massive amounts of wealth can be created and accumulated with virtually no substantial investment in physical assets. But the business cannot even get off the ground without considerable "sweat equity" from talented individuals working toward a common goal. It is now about "mind power."

Further proof lies in the fact that some of these businesses are not recreations of existing models, but completely new ways of doing business native to the Internet. We are no longer simply micro-improving old ideas to make a new enterprise or product better, faster or cheaper. Been there, done that. Enterprising minds of today are creating completely new business models and ways of interacting with clients never thought of before. Many more future services are yet to evolve that we can only dream about today. This creativity spurt will unleash new sources of wealth based on 'harnessing' creativity and ideas, not exploiting physical infrastructure or labour.

We should also consider the timelines in which this wealth is created. It is far easier to take advantage of the promise of an enterprising idea today, with less requirement for steep investments in physical infrastructure, than it has ever been in the past. This has allowed more and more people to access the means of wealth creation (their minds) and to rapidly create wealth for themselves rather than being dependent on others' wealth in the form of wages.

In our view, this trend will accelerate, offering people more choice about where and when they work and with whom they partner to share their valuable store of knowledge and creativity. This is the essence of the talent war so often talked about, a true shift in the power balance of the labour market. Workers in future will truly own their means of production and expect to share in wealth they create for others. We believe granting ownership to all employees, rather than simply founding executives, is an early sign of this hypothesis' credibility. But we do not yet find most corporations are benevolent enough to actively share the spoils of wealth creation with all their workers unless forced to do so by economic and competitive forces, a fact we find unfortunate.

Finally, let us consider the shareholder's role in all this. In the past, appetite for capital among businesses relying on physical infrastructure led to a competitive market where those with surplus cash could invest in organizations by buying shares and then demanding extraordinary returns for the use of their capital. The mechanics of this concept as played out in the world's major stock markets creates a desire in management to please shareholders in the short term. This often has an unduly negative influence on long-term thinking in many publicly traded companies. On the other hand, privately controlled enterprises were often run for the benefit of one or at most, a few shareholders, and lacked the unique financial focus of a widely held public company. Neither solution was perfect, but market forces offered at least some semblance of balance.

Today, capital is no longer the scarce resource it once was. Supply often exceeds demand. The stark reality for investors is that businesses need less cash to generate profits than in the past. This has changed the investor's role from simply lending capital to finding new ways of deploying capital to create wealth. This shift has seen the steady rise of private investment funds and "angel investors" who seek to secure early partnerships with those whose ideas they think will generate wealth by encouraging them not only with investment capital, but through access to experience, contacts and competitive or strategic insights. Smart investors today bring capital *and* knowledge to the table; they use this combination to generate expected returns.

The good news is that increased competitiveness for capital may bring a new level of respect for workers' creativity and contribution, helping restore a focus on long-term relationships rather than short-term returns. Just as we attached a premium to well capitalized enterprises in the past, we will in future attach a premium to enterprises that successfully reap the harvest of knowledge. Intellectual capital will drive the future economy, changing forever the notion of investors and investing.

What are the implications of all this? We believe soul-inspiring organizations will reap rewards simply as a result of their approach to inspiring people. The attractiveness of working together with others to build a world-class business will still dominate the thinking of many and lure them to employment. But, this will always come with an expectation of sharing the wealth they help create. It will also finally eliminate the need for businesses to think they need to manage people. Employees will be self-managing, choosing to stay or go based on their degree of commitment to employers' essential ideas and positive environments, rather than relying on them for wages. There will be mass movement toward self-actualization where people focus on the soft rewards of work as much as on salaries, since they will now share in long-term wealth creation as part of their overall compensation.

This significant shift will have a resounding impact on leadership practices. The call to true soul-inspiring leadership will be more important than ever, for the scrutiny and expectations of talented knowledge workers will naturally demand new heights of achievement as leaders focus on unleashing the collective creativity of their organizations. The outcome of successfully doing this will be to create new wealth for everyone in the enterprise. The interests of shareholders, leaders and employees will be closely aligned. Those that choose to malign or ignore any of these important groups' interests will pay the ultimate price—failing to secure their necessary share of intellectual and financial capital required to build their business in increasingly competitive arenas.

As companies' economic fortunes come to increasingly depend on these new forces of wealth creation, we will witness the continued rise of soul-inspiring workplaces, not as simply the "employers of choice" but as the "only acceptable choice" for employment! There will be no alternative.

QUESTIONS FOR REFLECTION

- How will the trend toward knowledge workers play out in your industry, and how does it impact you already?
- How do you see management practices/thinking as changing to acknowledge how important people are to the future creation of wealth?
- How does your personal wealth impact your thinking about the 'radical' ideas we are presenting?

DO'S AND DON'TS

- Do shift your emphasis from wealth accumulation (a physical assets model) to wealth creation (a knowledge management model).
- Do realize intellectual capital will drive the future economy, and prepare for that reality now.

- **Do** act on what you know about employees' expectations to share the wealth.
- **Do not** focus your compensation plan just on salaries without also attending to the soft rewards of work.
- **Do not** deny the mass movement toward self-actualization that is happening in your workforce.

EXERCISE FOR TEAM LEARNING

Proactively conduct an analysis of your industry. Consider the major tenets of this chapter as they relate to business models, the importance of knowledge workers, and the role of leaders and investors as stewards of intellectual capital. Use your analysis to develop clear ideas about the strategy and structure of winning enterprises in your sector. Map existing players against your criteria to determine who appears to be an "early adopter." Initiate a one-on-one conversation with your company's President/CEO to get his or her views of your analysis and jointly determine ways you can bring this information to your next leadership team meeting for action.

FIRST STEPS ALONG THE WAY

Assigned Task	*Expected Outcome*
Consider your current employer or company. Does it truly exhibit traits that would attract valuable knowledge workers? If so, identify the five strongest selling points in your view. If not, identify the five biggest barriers preventing you from attracting this resource to your firm. What can you do about this?	*Develops a realistic view of your current prospects in a competitive labour market where talent increasingly gravitates to inspiring and satisfying workplaces.*
Assume that you had exactly $1,000,000 to invest for your future retirement. How much of this would you feel safe investing in your organization today? If not one hundred percent, then how much and why? If none, why? If you invested less than one hundred percent, what would have to happen with your organization for you to change your mind? How can you contribute to making these changes happen more quickly because your investment thoughts probably match those of many other investors? If you won't invest, why should they?	*When we think of our organization's resources as "ours" rather than as "theirs," we begin to achieve a different image of our responsibility to be good stewards of the wealth we already have and our responsibility to generate more wealth in future. As leaders, we must not shy away from this basic concept and we must be prepared to create, secure and re-invest intellectual and social capital that will help improve rates of return on invested capital.*

X-traordinary

> **To thine own self be true...**
>
> —Shakespeare

It's all about you. "*I knew it!*" you reply with self-satisfied glee. Delighted, you imagine how everyone and everything should and does revolve around you. You imagine that direct reports exist solely to pay homage to you, as if they were all highly paid extras in your personal movie. You fall in love with the idea that your workforce hangs on your every word. And when you command them to "*Jump!*" their automatic response is, "*How high?*" Wouldn't this be a grand world indeed, one in which it would be worthwhile to get up for work in the morning?

Pop! That was the sound of your fantasy bubble bursting. *Whoosh*. That was the sound of all that hot air releasing. Disappointment or relief? What was your reaction to our sudden intrusion into your 'ideal' managerial world?

In the real world of 'x-traordinary' leadership, it is absolutely all about you. The extra that transforms ordinary leadership into 'x-traordinary' is you. You are the ingredient that makes a difference in the leadership mix—just not in the way we had you imagine. The genius of genetics is to create each of us as different and distinct, all with traits that are both a result of nature and nurture. As you have no doubt already concluded, we embrace and celebrate this uniqueness and feel that the quintessential nature of being human is to be unique.

While one eye remains on the 'I' (and the importance of their own uniqueness), notice that ultimately 'x-traordinary' leaders are more interested in 'we'—as in generating an environment where we (read: everyone) are cherished for our true selves. To accomplish this end, they know all roads unquestionably lead back to being real; soul-inspiring leaders accept full responsibility for the fact that greater authenticity at work starts with them. They profoundly believe that the more of themselves everyone brings through the door (i.e., who they really are), the broader will be the overall workplace. By broader, we mean a workplace where 'x-traordinary' leaders model sincerity and truthfulness, thereby encouraging others to do the same. When the workplace is broad, we invite everyone to offer his or her whole self to the task at hand, which inevitably translates into greater productivity, creativity and profitability.

'X-traordinary' leaders are not afraid to show their true colours. While typical managerial advice counsels not to get too close to associates, true leaders realize openness is a necessary ingredient to being fully trusted. This implies disclosure—not about your darkest secrets—but about who lives within your interior. Granted, personal disclosure feels highly risky. We cannot be certain colleagues will appreciate our candor, buy into our aspirations, or interpret our words and actions in the spirit they are meant. Through their willingness to take such risks, real leaders encourage employees to reciprocate. For, if neither party takes some authentic risks, the development of a deeper relationship remains stalled. In being first to ante up, 'x-traordinary' leaders take the critical first steps to create a culture founded on interpersonal trust and genuine collaboration.

They recognize that any time you live behind a mask, unseen and unknown by others, you are not putting your authentic self forward. You are able to allow only partial and selective glimpses into who you really are, afraid of the consequences of others knowing you fully. Intimacy in relationships becomes defined as those who are allowed to get a little closer to the truest part of who you are. But often, nobody is allowed right into the centre. You live in a terrifying world of secrets and false identities. There are bound to be some barriers to true intimacy in settings in which these masks are used. The consequence of this is to perpetuate a view of the leader internally and externally that is not authentic... as is the case with the next two examples that come to mind.

Both share in common an almost palpable feeling of withholding when one interacts with these individuals, particularly when it comes to hearing what they are actually thinking or feeling. With Martha, it often feels as though she is holding some sort of ace close to her chest, so that one can never really ascertain her true motives. Leaving others guessing has the effect of dissipating energy and having them wish she would for once trust enough to share her full 'deck.' Martha's withholding breeds mistrust—the opposite of the trusting atmosphere engendered through authenticity.

With the other, all is always rosy in Mark's world, no matter how much chaos seems to swirl around him. So, what's the problem with that? You may be thinking, "*I wish we had more like him on my team. What a great attitude.*" If that is what you are thinking, you are missing a key distinction. It is one thing to remain grounded when all around you are seemingly losing their heads. That is a positive trait, and thank goodness there are people like that. It is quite another when the unintended impact of the leader's almost unnatural optimism is to deny the truth of the situation around him. This is the subtlety we are pointing to.

Particularly for team members who have a high personal value set around speaking out, Mark's ultra-optimism actually shuts down more authentic communication. These employees who speak up know they will inevitably come away from conversations with him either frustrated or demoralized from being made wrong for pointing out all is not well. While not as devastating as being punished outright for speaking the truth, this lack of complete authenticity does leech away enthusiasm over time—at a minimum. Even if lauded by senior management for his cheerfulness (and Mark is), rest assured that his employees' experience is more like: "*If only he would just acknowledge the insanity for once, then we could do something about it.*"

To do any effective problem solving—something in which he expresses a great deal of interest and something which these team members are also after—you have to first recognize there is a problem. With both leaders, we would like to give them a tap on the back, like a baby being burped, to encourage them to finally "spit out" something authentic! We think it would make a huge difference in how they and others respond to one other.

We recognize that the argument against this level of openness is that we make ourselves vulnerable. Rather than being frightened, 'xtra-ordinary' leaders treat vulnerability as a strength. Comfortable with showing their own imperfections, they see this as fabric binding people together. This concept is easy to understand in theory, but less obvious when put into practice. When leaders we coach start to open up, we have witnessed time and again an initial reaction around them of stunned disbelief. This level of authenticity, especially in the workplace, is not common. People frequently need a period of time to adjust to this style and understand how genuine your vulnerability is. But, this change has its rewarding results.

By exposing some vulnerability, leaders merely demonstrate their approachability and trustworthiness. Consider the example of three leaders presenting at a half-day session with impatient executives in the audience. One speaker was highly nervous about his English, admitting he would be difficult to understand. By sharing his weakness right up front, this charming character invited the group to set aside their usual critical tendencies. Quite possibly, it was simply revealing his human foibles that so endeared him. Either way, he received a round of applause more vociferous than the other two speakers combined!

This is what revealing your authentic self is all about—letting followers see you are both human and humane. A key point, if you are going to be 'x-traordinary.' People must see that there is a person, a human being, behind their leaders, or they will not be comfortable revealing their own true selves. They must also see evidence of your ability to be compassionate. If this is not present, they will hide their realness. Everyone then loses because a part of each individual was left at the company gate.

Of course, showing vulnerability requires circumspection. For example, we would never suggest exposing a weakness that would jeopardize your professional role. This is merely opening oneself up to scorn and other negative outcomes. Done properly, self-disclosure builds solidarity between followers and leaders. 'X-traordinary' leaders therefore continuously reflect on the question: "*Did I show up fully for work today or did only part of me make it?*"

In order to be 'x-traordinary' at work, leaders must look at the totality of their lives. It requires unleashing your spirit into all parts of your life, including your workplace. This level of openness and genuineness not only describes qualities we are. Almost like an active verb, being 'x-traordinary' is something we do. It is a commitment to live with personal honour. When modeled by a leader who drops the mask first, the result is genuine interaction. True leadership is a relationship where one can be vulnerable enough to share one's deepest self and only become more human in the process.

Unlike the volumes prescribing mechanistic steps for becoming a clone of famous leaders, we can provide no universal formulas for increasing your ability to be 'x-traordinary.' By definition, attaining soul-inspiring leadership demands a continuous, dedicated process where you tune in to your particular genius, and use these gifts to derive a personal style that works for you. We cheer you on in applying what you learn by unashamedly revealing to others who you are under all the layers. After all, nobody can be you like you... and that is 'x-traordinary'!

QUESTIONS FOR REFLECTION

- How would you describe your real self—who you are when no one is looking?
- To what degree would you say your associates really know you—right to the extent of them introducing you as their friend?
- Ask yourself: "*Why would anyone want to be led by me?*"

DO'S AND DON'TS

- **Do** get comfortable showing your own imperfections and realize this is a thread binding people together.
- **Do** share with followers that you are both human and humane.
- **Do not** be afraid to reveal your authentic and genuine self.
- **Do not** feel you need to disclose your deepest, darkest secrets.

EXERCISE FOR TEAM LEARNING

Choose up to ten colleagues whom you will 'interview' for five to ten minutes each to ask the question: "*What is your listening for me?*" They should represent a cross-section of your workforce (i.e., your leader, peers, direct reports, others with whom you regularly communicate). The question is purposely broad. Try not to clarify it too much. If you must explain, add that you are asking about their thoughts and feelings when you interact with them. Invite them to be candid. Indicate you will be bringing your distilled notes to your next team meeting to share with direct reports. At your next team meeting, review what you will start, stop and keep doing as a leader (especially around being 'x-traordinary') based on others' feedback. Ask for their help in holding you to your commitments. This exercise can be extended to your entire team by having everyone complete the process and then summarizing with one another what they learned.

FIRST STEPS ALONG THE WAY

Assigned Task	*Expected Outcome*
How authentic do you allow yourself to be at work with others? Determine what action steps you can personally take to increase your ability to be vulnerable in work situations.	*Awareness is the first step to resolving an issue. Just noticing your own degree of self-expression increases consciousness around often sub-conscious behaviour patterns.*
Read Debbie Ford's book, *The Secret of the Shadow*. Take a personal inventory of what you would call your "shadow" self and examine the traits you can and cannot stand to be around.	*Opening up these parts in you creates the possibility for others to do the same. The greater the range of personalities you can relate to successfully at work, the less likely your 'buttons' are to be pushed. You are also less likely to get caught up in your own mind games when talking to people.*
At your next meeting, disclose something about yourself that others don't know. We are not talking deep dark secrets here, just something that enables others to get to know you a little better and makes you more open to them.	*Openness leads to trust, and trust is essential to authenticity across the workplace. Role modeling by taking this step first encourages others to do the same. Lays the groundwork for having colleagues reveal more of themselves.*

Yearning

> **A rock pile ceases to be a rock pile the moment a single man contemplates it, bearing within himself the image of a cathedral.**
>
> —Antoine de Saint-Exupery

Have you ever wondered why most heart attacks occur at nine o'clock on Monday morning? If we are honest, is this not how many of us view our work world—never-ending slavery that only ceases once we are liberated through retirement (or a good outplacement package)? Why else do so many people call in 'sick' on Monday or Friday morning? We believe the sheer number of you who are shaking your heads in acknowledgement of the distress involved in dragging yourself to work each day supports our theory of work as an often soul-deadening experience.

For so many, their daily working lives may regrettably be described by a quote from W.S. Gilbert: "*Did nothing in particular and did it very well*"! Disengaged, the soul yearns for something more. This longing to make a difference is fundamental to our core need as humans. It is part of our eternal search for meaning and also why W.S. Gilbert's statement is so heartbreaking—it directly opposes everything we know about the human condition.

Particularly in our coaching practices, we cannot begin to count how many people ask us to help them create more purposeful lives. As a result, much of our personal coaching is about helping others unleash their full potential. People want to know their lives matter in some way; that their presence on Earth has meaning.

Consistently, we find their greatest sense of fulfillment comes through the opportunity to serve others or to improve the world in some way. In a workplace context, this something more for which people pine is typically expressed as yearning for a lofty vision and uncompromising values. For those of you who may be protesting, "*But I, as an employer, do not owe people a sense of meaning. If that's what they need, then they should find it outside of work hours, on their own time,*" we have some 'bad' news for you. If that is your philosophy, then you must also accept your organization is operating at a fraction of its potential due to your failure to engage what is most important to your employees. There is a measurable and real cost to this suboptimal level of performance.

Take the example of one workplace. A long-term employee left the firm, fatigued by years of devoted service that saw Jim over and over work weekends and stay until after midnight to crank out production, all in the name of being a good 'team player' who helps the company pull out of the hat magical solutions that "*never miss a deadline.*"

For over seven years, receiving overflowing praise from the firm's founder each time Jim had been a 'good trooper' was actually enough to satisfy his yearning to make a contribution. Over time, continuously rescuing his employers from chaos at the sacrifice of his own goals ceased to have 'meaning.' Slowly, Jim stood up for himself, refusing at one point to surrender his long weekend to deal with yet another emergency. By the next business day, he was barely acknowledged by this same owner who had previously praised him limitlessly. How quick is the fall from grace! From then until his actual resignation, Jim retaliated by taking out his 'attitude' on those around him. In effect, he had resigned on the job. Colleagues felt the impact by having to pick up Jim's slack and became demoralized from his constant complaining. The 'hard' costs of this unfortunate situation were in the form of decreased production while he was still earning a full salary and increased rework as his lack of caring now resulted in expensive mistakes that took extra effort by others to fix.

We are glad for Jim's courage in finally answering that nagging inner voice calling out to him for some while, reminding him of the change he really wanted to make. We are certain he feels reinforced in his decision to restore a sense of meaning to his life by leaving. Behind Jim are numerous others—employees who have already left, if not physically, then emotionally, mentally and spiritually. Even as emails lauding the latest Herculean effort continue to circulate in that environment, so many yearn in their heart of hearts for some bigger possibility for their lives.

And that is the tragic part. All these people anxious to leave would not be 'necessary,' if only the firm's owners realized that the way they do business is at cause for both their internal problems and their lackluster results in the marketplace. The two go hand-in-glove. Sadly, they believe that visions about return-on-investment, monopoly-sized market percentages and jumps in customer satisfaction ratings actually resonate with people's souls. They truly feel rallying under crisis sparks passionate commitment from employees to achieve the impossible. Although it would surprise these owners, we assert that typical business accomplishments as measured by profit-based goals are inadequate to satisfy most people's yearning for a sense of meaning in their work.

Humans were not created singularly for the pursuit of material success, nor should we measure our life's value by our careers. Unfortunately, many of us do just that. It is somehow so easy to be seduced by the thought that a meaningful life will result if we only work harder and earn more. As in the example, many organizations take this for granted. They assume that by offering enough money or praise for superhuman efforts, they will satisfy employees' deepest yearnings. Like the founder in our example, many leaders are so consumed by corporate beliefs that they too have lost perspective on what a meaningful life can and should be. They have sold out. And they often rightly assume you will follow them!

We are not saying that in the soul-inspiring workplace, money is not an essential ingredient. In fact, earning an acceptable living is fundamental to feeling successful. But this ingredient should not replace leaders' desire to help employees lead meaningful lives. You cannot buy your way to meaning either, or choose to pay more and then expect to extract employees' last drop of blood. A nourished soul requires a meaningful life. We cannot forever be distracted from the whispers of our true soul's purpose by the constant lure of the "siren song of materialism." Rather, soul-inspiring leaders create meaning and in turn reap the rewards from committed employees grateful to the organization for helping them achieve it.

If you really want to put these points into perspective, we challenge you to find one person lying on their deathbed who wishes they had spent more time at the office—even the most seriously addicted workaholic! We are sure, many do lie on their deathbed wishing they had led more meaningful lives. There is more proof today than ever that these values are re-emerging. "Generation X," the first of our time to have been raised mostly as latchkey children by full-time "working moms," displays a consistent backlash against the values of their parents' generation. They watched as both parents spent years toiling in organizations only to be cast out in re-engineering blitzes later in life. They experienced the emotional pain of essential abandonment as two-career families tried to balance raising children and working full time. They watched the steady increase in hours spent at the office pursuing promotions to the sacrifice of everything meaningful. Now they are righting what they see as lack of balance between working and living. They see work as a means to an end and are prepared to end it if it does not offer the means! This is a dramatic shift in collective values.

Only organizations that can adapt to these emerging demands will be able to recruit and retain the young talent they need to survive. Yet, so many older managers today do not share a common view of what is meaningful with this new generation, setting up a serious conflict. The conflict is not really about skills or productivity. Each group has these. The younger generation may even have an advantage, having grown up in a technologically advanced world and with more of a global view than any previous generation. So what is the issue? That the new generation will only work in soul-inspiring organizations—ones that help them create meaningful lives as they define them, not as previous generations have come to define it.

Consider the possibilities if we viewed "business" as the Swedes do. In their language, it translates into "nourishment for life." What a different way to hold the meaning of work than as back-breaking drudgery. What if work gave expression to employees' deepest yearnings, rather than being a slow killer of their spirits? Imagine if the outcome of people's efforts was potential exploded across the organization. What if we could transform work from stagnation to inspiration and exhilaration? We firmly believe these are not just pipe dreams but real possibilities for how work can show up in our lives and for how we can show up at work.

Soul-inspiring leaders profoundly realize this. They know millions are pleading through a universal cry for meaning, purpose and character in organizational life. They answer this cry by contributing to the pursuit of meaning within a work context, so that time spent can be seen as making a difference rather than as mindless. They create workplaces where the deepest human needs are met. They answer people's yearning to work in settings where they find fulfillment that contributes to their quest for a meaningful existence.

QUESTIONS FOR REFLECTION

- How would you answer the question: "My life is meaningful because…"?
- List the accomplishments in your life to date of which you are most proud, noting how many involve work. Are there too few or too many in this category, and what does this mean to you?
- If you learned you had three months to live, in what ways would you reorganize your life? If you would make changes, what is stopping you from living with this sense of meaning now, with your 'whole' life ahead of you?

DO'S AND DON'TS

- **Do** remember that employees' yearning has to do with making a difference through serving or improving the world in some way.
- **Do** realize that failure to engage what is most important to employees does come with the price tag of operating at suboptimal performance levels.
- **Do** bear in mind, when recruiting young talent needed for survival, the backlash demonstrated by "Generation X," who are not prepared to sacrifice meaning for a paycheque.
- **Do not** see yearning as complaining.
- **Do not** believe that lauding superhuman efforts alone creates meaning and answers people's deepest yearnings.

- **Do not** think you can pay more and in return expect to extract employees' last drop of blood.

EXERCISE FOR TEAM LEARNING

Find a comfortable place in which you can quietly reflect and write. This is a deeply introspective exercise, so you will want to make sure you have enough undisturbed thinking time. Imagine you get to attend your own funeral. Now write down what you would like people to say about you. Describe in detail what you want to have your life stand for. Describe what you did that other people remembered even after you died. Describe who you were and what you valued most in life. Write your own eulogy, and then consider what you learned from this process. This exercise can be done individually by your team members, and then shared one by one as part of a team-building retreat. We have done it as a group exercise, to great success.

FIRST STEPS ALONG THE WAY

Assigned Task	*Expected Outcome*
Read or re-read *Man's Search for Meaning* by Viktor Frankl. A profound book set against the backdrop of Nazi Germany, it describes the impact of concentration camp life on a psychiatrist's understanding of the true meaning of life.	*Teaches us that if someone like Frankl could live his life to the fullest under extraordinarily difficult circumstances, then so too can we learn to follow our dreams under much less trying conditions.*
Establish a simple 'Life Plan.' What will define you in life? How will it be accomplished? How and when will your dreams become goals?	*Promotes important reflection on meaningful life questions. Generates clarity as to the way you want to create each day and therefore the legacy by which you will ultimately be known.*
Assume if you cannot create an organization that addresses employees' yearning for meaning, you will eventually fail. What would you have to change that would make your company a place where people yearn to work? Determine what you would need to keep, start and stop doing (i.e., specific actions and behaviours) and take action.	*Uses your influence to help your organization obtain the kind of people-practices advantage it will need to stay competitive.*

Zap

> **The brain is a wonderful organ. It starts working the moment you get up in the morning, and does not stop until you get into the office.**
>
> **—Robert Frost**

We believe the only people policy any organization needs is this: use your own best judgment and do what is right for the customer and company. Or, you may substitute your own clear version that would guide every employee's actions in all situations. Now that we likely have policy writers everywhere up in arms, permit us to stretch the envelope even farther by asserting, we believe policies are nothing other than "scar tissue on an error"! We unequivocally find most policies and procedures manuals exist solely because one employee made one error at one time (usually early in the company's history) that forever after casts all others in this individual's wake as incompetents who must now be told precisely what to do, how to do it and when to do it. As if designing the perfect Rule Book could absolutely guarantee no errors are ever made again!

The very words and syllables policy writers slave over for hours are the very cause of soured attitudes, dried-up motivation, resignation, anger and worse. For, when otherwise productive and innovative people become buried under top-heavy bureaucracies and unreasonable regulations, we squeeze the lifeblood out of the exact qualities organizations need for long-term survival.

If one truly seeks to build ingenuity and resourcefulness, does it not make more sense to focus our efforts on creating cultures that eliminate these inane restrictions? Or, as we often say, just "*zap 'em.*" Then create only policies that grant the latitude needed for superior performance. Imagine what is possible if we give people the freedom to perform in ways that energize and engage their very best skills and talents.

This brings to mind the fabled story of the elephant, whose cruel owner once shackled it to a mooring easily destroyed through brute force alone. Punished often enough for struggling to get free, the fatigued animal eventually surrendered its fighting spirit in hopelessness. It remained rooted to the spot long after its fastenings were removed, even though it was free to roam around. Like our elephant, many employees have had the painful experience of being beaten down while they, too, were spirited 'animals.' When this happens they give up even trying to offer their employers any inventiveness or creative spark. "*What's the point?*" they question. "*We'll only get shot down anyway.*"

In under-performing workplaces, we call this the "inertia of cultural resistance." This dynamic played out in an organization in which we once consulted, but it is recognizable in a number of contexts. A new employee took over leadership of two individuals who had reported to one of these elephant-like managers. The previous manager, Lucy, instilled such a narrow mindset over the years that she wound up transferring her blinders to her former charges, rendering them virtually incapable of thinking for themselves. Now enter the new leader, Patricia—invigorated and invigorating, committed to reigniting employees' enthusiasm. What do you suppose happened? Her new direct reports loved Patricia and the other administrative staff secretly wanted to report to her. Why? She went to bat for her people. Everyone knew she stood for others' greatness. Not surprisingly, some managers were deeply threatened by the breath of fresh air Patricia blew into the environment, because they knew they could no longer resort to their old ways of controlling direct reports in the face of this soul-inspiring leader. We know high loyalty ensues when people feel deep personal commitment to their leaders and it is precisely every single individual's contributions that will be needed to support companies' growth in future. Leaders will soon have no choice but to surrender their elephant-like ways!

In our experience, soul-inspiring environments do not happen by accident, but rather through a set of dedicated actions designed to build an extraordinary workplace. First, leaders cannot suddenly wave a wand and declare: "*You are now accountable.*" Such abdication of responsibility is as dangerous as over-control. Actually, both are flip sides of the same coin. It is the difference between one leader who used accountability to scapegoat, and our philosophy to encourage team members to take on greater responsibility through gradual delegation, training and coaching. Without authority to make business decisions, employees will shun accountability.

Our final Simple Leadership Equation says it best:

SIMPLE LEADERSHIP EQUATION #9:

Accountability = Authority

Both sides of this equation must be equal and you can never achieve one without the other. Expecting accountability without giving authority is an impossibility!

Second, the organization's systems (both informal and those formalized through planning, structuring, recruiting, selecting, hiring, training, rewarding, communicating, decision-making, etc.) must be aligned to support vision and values. In our experience, inconsistencies between high-performance business objectives and corporate rules of the game are a major inhibitor to workplace transformation. And, if you are still determined to have policies and procedures, at least make sure they are fair and administered even-handedly. Better yet, though, why not zap those rules by tossing them out altogether? Why not create from a blank slate a set of Philosophy Statements delineating how you want to treat people and have them feel about their workplace? Spend your time reinforcing these. Here are some excerpts from the Rules of Engagement (the code which every employee agreed to live by) of the organization we were helping build:

- We respect people as contributors to the success of the enterprise, regardless of function, position, or title.
- We will not gossip, bitch or complain.
- We will not indulge in diminishing people's ideas by sarcasm or ridicule.
- If we have done any damage in our communications, we will clean it up within twenty-four hours.

Although this is only a sample, the words serve to powerfully indicate to the reader the boundaries of acceptable and unacceptable behaviour in plain language terms.

Third, like it or not, leaders' own words and actions are the make-it or break it ingredient in this zapping mix. Empowering leaders see themselves more as coaches and champions than as controllers and decision makers. It really boils down to a self-fulfilling prophecy: if we expect the best from others, they will probably succeed. Employees' self-talk is absolutely reinforced by leaders, so why not make certain it comes from positive actions like taking time to develop, coach and reward. A worthy ultimate goal is to create a self-directed work team capable of taking full ownership of their jobs, including goal-setting and performance management. The leader's role then becomes one of providing guidance and support by paving the way for new initiatives, clearing roadblocks and generating senior-level commitment. This is the kind of leadership that inspires everyone's souls.

In the end, empowerment is not something you do to people, though it is often defined and executed as such. We suspect this is why it gets a bad name. Empowerment is nurtured by creating an environment like that of a hotel we know. Every employee is supported to do what it takes to satisfy guests. It is the difference between a car rental agency experience where our friend saw immediate proof from the service provider of actions to rectify her issues, and a financial institution that lost our mortgage business through the bank manager's unwillingness to address simple questions about renewing our arrangement. These examples illustrate the powerful connection between satisfied employees, contented customers and the bottom line.

While we are not claiming creating environments that free people is easy, surely the benefits outweigh the time and effort invested. Employees who "own their jobs" are motivated to do them well and isn't improved performance what it is all about in an organization? Think about the avalanche of energy and zest released by lifting the burden of hampering rules and regulations; the increased creativity, initiative and commitment are tangible. In our fast-moving, complex and changing world, high levels of positive emotional energy can be linked directly to faster cycle times, higher quality, lower costs and the ability to continuously transform. You need to get there to be competitive in today's global environment.

Given our view that a corporation's emotional energy level offers a prime competitive advantage, what do websites like "mybosssucks.com" say about the internal state of affairs in so many companies? In some ways, it is discouraging to note the number of disgruntled employees who seek this web-based outlet as the only safe means by which to vent about stupid bosses, expensive mistakes, brainless decisions and annoying habits. Especially when the antidote is as 'simple' as reframing our notions about people—by facilitating rather than limiting their innate desire to make a difference. As was so succinctly stated in one CEO presentation recently: "*A company is its people. Low energy people make for a low energy company.*" Do you zap what stands in their way or layer them up with soul restricting rules? It's up to you.

QUESTIONS FOR REFLECTION

- How would you describe your expectations of those you lead and how might that be influencing their performance?
- To what extent do you let your team decide on its own approach to assignments?
- How do you get in the way of your team? What can you do about this right now?

DO'S AND DON'TS

- **Do** encourage employees to use their own best judgment to do what is right for the customer and company.
- **Do** eliminate the "inertia of cultural resistance" by freeing people from restrictive rules and regulations.
- **Do** realize empowerment is not something you do *to* people, but that you do *with* people.
- **Do** facilitate, rather than limit, people's innate desire to make a difference.
- **Do not** fall into the trap of believing you can wave a magic wand and declare: "*You are now accountable.*"

- **Do not** view your leadership role as strictly controlling and decision making; do see yourself more as a coach and champion.

EXERCISE FOR TEAM LEARNING

Spend ten to fifteen minutes in your next team meeting brainstorming lists of organizational systems (formal and/or informal) that either support or hinder them. Next focus on three or four sources of restriction/burden you could directly eliminate or significantly influence. Answer these questions: What problem is this policy or regulation causing in our organization? What ideas do people have for turning these sources of disempowerment into sources of engagement? What actions would your team need to take to implement them? What are the barriers to implementing these ideas and how can you overcome them? What support will people need from their leader(s)? What are the first steps? Who will take them, and by when?

FIRST STEPS ALONG THE WAY

Assigned Task	*Expected Outcome*
Create a weekly Win Log that can be shared across the company. Rather than capturing unresolved problems, use it for successes. Each person could be invited to share at least one win at weekly team meetings. Equally, the current week's successes could be recorded on a whiteboard or colourful cards posted around the office. The nature of the win does not matter.	*Instead of continuously focusing on what is not working via Suggestion Systems, a Win Log encourages people to notice what is working and thereby reinforces ways the environment frees them to do their jobs. It is a great way of ensuring that in subsequent weeks people are looking for their successes.*
Read George Bernard Shaw's *Pygmalion* or rent the movie *My Fair Lady*.	*In showing the power of positive expectations, acts as a reminder that people align their behaviour with your expectations of them.*
Walk around your workplace, noticing images on the walls. Observe whether they communicate positive or negative messages. If it is the latter, invest in posting some inspirational images.	*Using this vehicle invites people's enthusiasm and energy to become engaged by what they see around them. It also demonstrates through images the spirit you are promoting in your culture.*

The Challenge Ahead

It is often the case that most of us possess on some level a "fear of failure" that translates over time into a "fear of trying." Practicing soul-inspiring leadership is not easy, but it is also not impossible. It's just hard work. But all hard work has its just reward, and those who can embrace the ideals in this book will be happier and more fulfilled for having undertaken their own journey in discovering the power of soul.

As authors, we struggle with how to ensure that our message is hard-hitting while not negative. That we remain positive but also prescriptive. That we do not only identify problems, but offer solutions. However, at the end of the day, we can only open doors of knowledge rather than force you to walk though them. Yet it is our deepest hope in writing this book that we can help you turn our words into actions that create positive outcomes in your life.

One thing we have identified from the hundreds of workshops and speeches we have each given during our respective careers is that people like simple answers. As consultants, we rebel against this facile request and often do not believe that there are "simple solutions to complex problems." Yet, we often seem to arrive at a place where the solutions we offer, while complete and theoretically sound, are meaningless to our clients because they have a sense they are too complex. We do not want that to happen with this book and this was one of the primary reasons we focused on our nine Simple Leadership Equations as examples of making theory accessible. In the interests of simplicity and based on experience, we are going to offer another suggestion for some of you that may work to help you embrace a book like this.

OUR EQUATION FOR PERSONAL GROWTH:

26 Letter Chapters x 2 Weeks Each
= 1 Year Timeline to Change

Now that you have presumably read our book and hopefully felt the impact of our hypotheses, we challenge you to make a commitment for the year that lies ahead. Why not take each chapter and devote just two weeks to it? We recommend the first week would be spent re-reading the chapter at the beginning of the week and the rest of the week be spent in observation about your life in relation to the chapter. At the end of that week, make simple and precise commitments to yourself about what you are going to change ***within the following*** week that will start your own journey moving forward. If you do this for each chapter and do it consistently, we guarantee that at the end of one year your life will be very different. How is that for simple?

Simple you say. Yet, many of you will not do this. Or do anything. This book will be read and enjoyed for a moment or two, but it will not have any lasting impact on the way you act or behave. So while we can reflect on the challenge that lies ahead for many of us who "get it," the real problem is what to do about those among us who do not! What can one do when they find themselves forced to work in a toxic environment that is soul depleting rather than soul restoring? This is a question we are often asked by readers at our seminars and speeches. "*What can I do?*" they cry. "*I have no choice.*"

The challenge that lies ahead for any reader of this book is the ultimate recognition that you ***do*** have a choice. We all have choices. It is the will to execute that may be lacking because this "soul stuff" is darn hard work. The decision that work alone is not fulfilling your soul's purpose is a harsh realization that has many implications, none of which are easy to deal with. But, the challenge that lies ahead for you is in making the decision to actually act on your intentions and find or create a workplace that will allow your and others' souls to thrive, not dive. This is the real call to action of our book!

Recent global events have reminded all of us of the importance of human relationships. At the individual level, we believe that we are all created as social creatures with an innate desire to have satisfying, fulfilling relationships. Whether we consider this in a personal or a professional context, the implications are the same. *Effective relationships effectively feed our souls; ineffective relationships bleed our souls.* Therefore, the choice in terms of what we pursue for ourselves is the essence of a decision to be happy or not. Who would consciously choose not to be happy? Yet, how many of you choose to remain in workplaces that do not meet your expectations for soul-inspiring work? This is absolutely an essential life choice we must make: what is our purpose and how will we fulfill this destiny over time?

So, the challenge ahead is real. We acknowledge the enormity of the task, but we ask you to embrace this once-in-a-lifetime journey by making the decision to change the world, one little step at a time, one day at a time. Change your ways. Challenge others to change. Enable your organization to develop new perspectives that will help it to thrive. Live out your intention to be soul-inspiring and expect the same in others.

Our hope is that this book has been one minor contribution to a major shift in your thinking about the world and its potential for you. We walk with you in spirit on the journey and wish your soul well!

www.soul-inspiring-leadership.com

How's Your Current Workplace?

We recognize that for many of you, providing useful assessment tools might be helpful to implement the contents of our book. Therefore, the attached questionnaire is one that Carol-Ann uses quite a bit with clients to assess their workplace "spiritual health." As such, you may wish to apply it to your current workplace and determine how well you are doing!

QUESTIONNAIRE:

Indicate a number for each statement to express your level of agreement:

1 = Strongly Disagree **2** = Disagree **3** = Neutral **4** = Agree **5** = Strongly Agree

	1	2	3	4	5
1. I feel acknowledged by my leader and workplace.					
2. I am encouraged to balance work and other aspects of life.					
3. I express my convictions, without consequences.					
4. I am invited to offer diverse views from those of colleagues.					
5. I feel safe in demonstrating human emotions at work.					
6. I enjoy a sense of fun and camaraderie with my team and others.					
7. I am treated graciously when I fail.					
8. I apply both my heart and head when carrying out my duties.					
9. I bring the full range of my imagination to my role.					
10. I find my job allows me to be rewarded for contribution.					
11. I am sought out by my leader for what I know.					
12. I continue to learn and grow through my work.					
13. I find my leader brings a sense of maturity to our interactions.					
14. I see a balance between male and female perspectives at work.					

	1	2	3	4	5
15. I am constantly asked to eliminate the status quo.					
16. I feel enthused to bring my ideas and energy to all I do.					
17. I am encouraged to ask questions, at any organizational level.					
18. I spend time on both task and relationships at work.					
19. I experience my leader as someone who stands for my success.					
20. I find technology supports rather than hinders me.					
21. I am supported with skills and methods to deal with upheaval.					
22. I live high alignment between personal and organizational values.					
23. I believe my employer attracts knowledge workers.					
24. I am my authentic self at work, in all ways.					
25. I derive a sense of meaning and fulfillment from what I do.					
26. I am trusted for my judgment and ability to do the right thing.					
TOTALS:					

Add the numbers you marked.

What is your total score? ______

<30 Strong misalignment between you and your organization. Start asking yourself some important questions about whether this is the right place for you.

31–52 You are able to bring some of yourself to the workplace, but there is considerable room for improvement. Start identifying key missing elements to determine your direction.

53–78 You have taken steps to bring your whole self to work, but there is a way to go yet. What are the specific areas for improvement, and how can you create action within them?

79–104 Your work environment supports you to a strong degree. In the interests of continuous improvement, what are some remaining areas of focus and how can you make a difference in shifting these?

105+ Congratulations! You have found a workplace where you are able to live in a soul-inspiring way. Your spirituality is "alive and well" in your workplace.

WHAT IS WORK?

What is work
but a ceaseless taskmaster
a relentless slave driver
that coerces people into acts of self-destruction?

Or could work become
the unleashed expression of our deepest longings
potential exploded across the organization?

What is work
but an unyielding automaton
an unstoppable timepiece
that clocks only stellar accomplishments?

Or could work become
the quenched thirst for joy and wonder
"Happy Hour" expanded before 5:00 pm?

What is work
but an unpredictable chameleon
a devious politician
that destroys authenticity in the name of conformity?

Or could work become
the unbridled release of hearts and spirits
individuality treasured together with powerful connections?

What is work
but a bottom-line God

a capital oriented 'prophet'
that demands soul sacrifice in the name of the Almighty Dollar?

Or could work become
the answered call for unassailable values
competitive advantage sustained through principled leadership?

What is work
but a torture chamber,
a garbage disposal
that discards people when they can no longer serve?

Or could work become
the fine art of 'doing' while honouring human 'beings'
passion restored alongside double-digit productivity?

What is work
but desolation, stagnation, devastation?
Or could work become
inspiration, exhilaration, transformation?

Millions are seeking, yearning, pleading, questing, pining
through a universal cry
for meaning, purpose and character in business life.

We stand at the brink.
The choice is ours.